Strangers in a Foreign Land

Strangers in a Foreign Land

The Organizing of Catholic Latinos in the United States

George E. Schultze, SJ

LEXINGTON BOOKS

A division of
ROWMAN & LITTLEFIELD PUBLISHERS, INC.
Lanham • Boulder • New York • Toronto • Plymouth, UK

LEXINGTON BOOKS

A division of Rowman & Littlefield Publishers, Inc.
A wholly owned subsidiary of The Rowman & Littlefield Publishing Group, Inc.
4501 Forbes Boulevard, Suite 200
Lanham, MD 20706

Estover Road
Plymouth PL6 7PY
United Kingdom

British Library Cataloguing in Publication Information Available

Library of Congress Cataloging-in-Publication Data

Schultze, George E.
  Strangers in a foreign land : the organizing of Catholic Latinos in the United States /
George E. Schultze.
     p. cm.
  Includes bibliographical references and index.
  ISBN-13: 978-0-7391-1745-3 (cloth : alk. paper)
  ISBN-10: 0-7391-1745-9 (cloth : alk. paper)
  ISBN-13: 978-0-7391-1746-0 (pbk : alk. paper)
  ISBN-10: 0-7391-1746-7 (pbk : alk. paper)
  1. Church work with Hispanic Americans. 2. Hispanic American Catholics—
Religious life. I. Title.
  BX1407.H55S38 2007
  261.8'5—dc22   2006028904

Printed in the United States of America

∞™ The paper used in this publication meets the minimum requirements of
American National Standard for Information Sciences—Permanence of Paper
for Printed Library Materials, ANSI/NISO Z39.48-1992.

Contents

~

Acknowledgments

The analysis and views in this book are my own, but I am grateful to a num-ber of people who were willing to take a chance and allow me to voice some hopes and concerns with regard to the organizing of Catholic Latinos. Sheet Metal Workers' International Association Local No. 104 supported my ef-fort, and Financial Secretary/Treasurer Joseph A. Maraccini gave me the help and encouragement that I needed to see the book through to completion. The Sheet Metal Workers' International Association, Washington, D.C., also provided support and graciously invited me to observe its international convention in 2005. The United Association of Journeymen and Appren-tices of the Plumbing and Pipe Fitting Industry Local Union No. 38 and Business Manager/Financial Secretary Treasurer Larry J. Mazzola, Sr., helped me with the book's publication.

I wish to thank Wm. Craig Dobbs and the Dobbs family for their gener-ous gift as well as the Morton Foundation, whose gift was made in memory of Thomas A. Morton. I pray that this book will uphold their hopes for work-ers and their employers.

I greatly appreciate the professional support for editing and indexing given to me by Mary Tosi, Catherine Forrest Getzie, and June Sawyers.

I also give thanks to my fellow members of the Divine Mercy Eucharistic Society of the San Francisco Bay Area, especially the director, Thelma Orias.

Finally, I am dedicating this work to my father George, mother Annie, and brother John. Faith-filled working people who have been the salt of the earth for family, friends, co-workers, strangers, and me.

~

Introduction

When I began to write this book I knew that readers, in order to appreciate the contemporary organizing of Catholic Latinos, should learn something about the Roman Catholic Church's historical relationship with the labor movement in the United States. Today I see an opportunity for the labor movement to benefit from the Catholic Church's interest in the Catholic Latino immigrant population. Others have written extensively on the labor movement, the American Catholic Church, and the U.S. Latino population, but I want to provide a brief history of the relationship between the Church and labor with a focus on the importance of the involvement of the Church in the organizing of Latinos. I feel that for the uninitiated reader I would also provide a short explanation of the Christian tradition's understanding of labor, that is work, and some references to Catholic social teaching that address the question of labor. Again, I am not writing a full exposition of these themes. I only hope to provide sufficient background to help us begin to think more clearly about the economic organizing of Latinos given the role of work in all of our lives.

During many years of study, teaching, and pastoral work in California, I have had the opportunity to interview and develop working relationships with union members and leaders, union and nonunion Latino workers, community organizers, Catholic Church folk, and social activists. I value these relationships because as a Catholic priest I can make use of my vocation to promote the creation of good paying jobs, especially as one means of economic development within my home state of California and our nation. I have a particular affinity for Latinos because I am a Hispano, a Latino who can trace his American-born status back over the centuries (my mother's family—the Grijalva family—has been rooted in the southwest for hundreds of years). My father's family of good Irish, German, and Danish stock settled in California in the 1890s. Both families see themselves as American but are well aware of the journeying of their own forefathers, whether it was internal North American migration or European immigration.

I grew up in a union household in the San Francisco Bay area. Both my parents worked as union members in Santa Clara Valley fruit canneries, where my father was a shop steward. He later worked in a shingle factory as an International Longshore and Warehouse Union Local 6 member and then gravitated into construction and became a member of Operating Engineers Local 3. My mother was a member of the International Association of Machinists as a Lockheed Aerospace employee. She finished her work life as a quality control inspector in the unorganized Silicon Valley electronics industry, the remnants of which remain dependent on low-wage ethnic women to this day. Because of my parents' lives, I studied industrial and labor relations and worked as a Board Agent for the National Labor Relations Board before joining the Jesuit order. My interests have always centered on the subject of work life.

Although this book is not a definitive study of U.S. labor or Catholic Church history, it is an attempt to support Catholics and labor unionists who believe economic development in a society happens with work that provides a living wage. Unions have gained better wages, benefits, and improved working conditions for millions of workers, and the Church has supported this effort. The political and financial power of unions, however, can also work against the interests of the Catholic community. I use the cases of abortion and same-sex marriage as two issues that should not become a part of labor's agenda if Latinos, especially immigrant Catholic Latinos, are sought as union members and supporters. Readers are welcomed to take skeptical or opposing views of my analysis and arguments, but I hope my perspective may provide some fodder for more substantive work between the Catholic Church, labor, and employers in the United States. Although I cite national data on the Latino population and labor organizing—Latino immigration is obviously a national phenomenon—I am most interested in and familiar with the situation in California, which should be a good indicator for ongoing national trends concerning the organizing of Catholic Latinos. We might consider Los Angeles itself as a microcosm of America in the twenty-first century, and I point out the successes in organizing Latinos in Los Angeles.

The book is in English although one might think Spanish is the proper language for organizing Latinos who often are either monolingual in Spanish or bilingual. In fact, the American labor movement and American Catholic Church remain predominately English-speaking, and I am writing for English-speaking and bilingual organizers, union leaders, political staffers, and Catholic policymakers. Moreover, my review of literature suggests that we will continue to see the development of English as the first language of most Hispanics over time. The United States will not become a Spanish-speaking nation or even a bilingual nation.

One of my positions is that organizers, Church leaders, and politicians need to acknowledge and at some level respect those who intellectual elites might stereotypically call "brownnecks" (the Latino "redneck"), who undeniably make up a part of the Latino population, native and foreign born, in the United States. Their values and opinions may not be viewed as politically correct but are often born of faith and reason.

There are no political machines in today's urban centers but mediating institutions like the faith-based Pacific Institute for Community Organizations and the Industrial Areas Foundation can be found. These are good examples of community organizing groups that work successfully with Catholics because they are sensitive to Catholic moral and social teaching. If leaders of the various community and labor organizing groups are sympathetic to Catholic positions around key social issues or are at least neutral about them, I believe we will find more wins for working people than losses. Labor unions continue to fight an uphill battle but we need to encourage their presence because no democracy can exist without a viable labor movement. My hope is that this effort will contribute to that viability.

CHAPTER ONE

~

Aliens No More

Hispanic/Latino Demographics

I use Hispanic and Latino interchangeably and assume that most Americans realize we are not discussing a monolithic population. Some researchers have argued for a refined categorization of this political identity group because the backgrounds and socioeconomic status, which includes levels of education, are so different among its members. At this point in time most Americans recognize the differences. For example, Mexicans and Puerto Ricans as broadly identified most likely fit into the minority and low-income categories in the perspective of the majority of Americans. In some cases, individuals labeled as Hispanic or Latino have participated in American society for centuries and have not seen their numbers rise to the same standard of living as Americans of European descent. (In fact, some scholars would argue that when we speak of Latinos we are not speaking of immigrants but conquered and colonized peoples—"America" came to them.) Still other Hispanics/Latinos are more recent arrivals: Cuban, Central American, and South American refugees and immigrants. At times these immigrants have arrived with high levels of education and perhaps wealth while more often than not they have arrived with very little.[1] Latino immigrants often have Native American ancestry while some have primarily African-American and/or European ancestry. The United States as of 2002 had 37.4 million Latinos who made up 13.3 percent of the total population. On January 21, 2003, Hispanics became the largest minority group in the United States.

In 2000, 11 percent of the population in the United States was foreign born which was up from 5 percent in 1970. The wave of immigration to the United States in the last twenty years is visible in every city. The U.S. Census Bureau reports that 66.9 percent of the nation's "Hispanics" are Mexican, 14.3 percent are Central and South American, 8.6 percent are Puerto Rican, 3.7 percent are Cuban, and the remainder, 6.5 percent, are identified as other Hispanic.[2] Over 40 percent of the Latino population live in the West and over 30 percent reside in the South.[3] Central and South American immigrants have shown a tendency to move to the East, South, and West but less frequently to the Midwest. The Midwest, however, is presently experiencing the highest Hispanic population growth rates for any U.S. region. Clearly, Hispanics have fanned out throughout the entire country.

Latinos are more heavily concentrated in central cities of metropolitan areas (45.6 percent) than non-Latino whites (21.1 percent). Recent census data confirms what many of us already know from observation, that the Hispanic population is a younger population with 34.8 percent now under the age of eighteen as compared to 22.8 percent of the non-Hispanic population. If traveling in any major urban center and visiting the Latino barrio—e.g., Echo Park in Los Angeles, Pilsen and Little Village in Chicago, or Kalorama Heights and Adams Morgan in Washington, D.C., Latinos can be observed pushing baby strollers and directing young children. Within the Latino population itself, Mexicans have the highest percentage of young people, 37.1 percent under eighteen, and Cubans have the lowest number, 19.6 percent.[4]

All Americans need to remember that over half of all U.S. Latinos—59.8 percent—are native-born. Conversely, foreign-born Latinos make up 40.2 percent of all U.S. Hispanics, which without a doubt is a significant figure and a concern when many immigrants arrive with little financial or educational capital. Roughly half of the foreign-born arrived on U.S. soil during the past decade, a quarter came during the 1980s and about 20 percent arrived prior to 1980. Probably less than a third of the foreign-born Latinos who have arrived in the United States since 1970 have become citizens.[5]

The Latino population in the United States has larger than average households, fewer divorces, lower than normal high school graduation rates, and less wealth than other racial/ethnic groups. In 2002, 26.5 percent of Latino households had more than five members while 10.8 percent of non-Hispanic white households had five or more members. Ten percent of the non-Hispanic whites have been divorced while 6.6 percent of the Hispanics have ended their marriages. Many Hispanics have not obtained sufficient education to compete in today's global job market, and fully 43 percent of Hispanics over twenty-five have not graduated from high school. Only 11.3 percent of the non-Hispanic white population has failed to complete high school. In addition, one out of four Latinos has not finished the ninth grade. And while over a quarter of the non-Hispanic whites over twenty-five have graduated from college, only 11.1 percent of the Hispanics have achieved this American dream.

Unemployment figures continually show higher unemployment among Latinos than among non-Latino whites. In 2002, 8.1 percent of the Latinos over the age of sixteen were jobless, but the figure had dropped to 6.0 percent by 2005. The non-Latino white unemployment figure has remained steadily lower than that of Latinos; it was 5.1 percent in 2002 and 4.4 percent in 2005. Latinos have often been employed in service work and operator/laborer roles (22.1 percent and 20.8 percent, respectively). Comparable rates for non-Latino whites were 11.6 percent and 10.9 percent in 2002. Non-Latino whites worked more often in managerial positions (35.1 percent) than Latinos (14.2 percent). Finally, the national poverty rate for Hispanics was 21.4 percent and for non-Hispanic whites 7.8 percent.[6] National statistics unquestionably point to American Latinos as a low-income, working-poor population.

The population of Latinos in California is close to 32.4 percent; in Illinois, 12.3 percent; New York, 15 percent; and Washington, D.C., 7.9 percent. Hispanic day workers, house cleaners, and busboys are as prevalent as the ever-present Mexican restaurants in our American communities. We see both workers and their services as contributors to the U.S. standard of living. While the restaurants provide an international culinary experience for us all, the Hispanic worker carries flesh, blood, and spirit. Latinos, and in particular the Latinos who have established themselves in the United States in the last forty years, require a living wage to keep mind and body whole. They are striving to improve their lives and while some have met with success, others still need economic justice in making a better life for themselves.

The location of home and work helps us better understand the impact of these neighbors, friends, co-workers, and native-born Americans who are unwelcome foreigners. For example, in Los Angeles, the number of Latinos as a percentage of the population increased from 22 percent in 1970 to 54 percent in 2000. As a percentage of those living in poverty, Latinos made up 22 percent of those Angelenos in poverty in 1970 and 54 percent in 2000.[7] First-generation immigrants have settled in the inner city of Los Angeles proper, but the number of poor neighborhoods in the surrounding suburban areas of Los Angeles County has quadrupled since 1970.[8] The data shows that these poor areas are ethnically mixed but with a preponderance of Hispanics. The major cause of this increase in Hispanic poor living in Los Angeles is the legal and illegal immigration into the area. While Hispanics have moved into low-income neighborhoods, poor and very poor,[9] the percentage of African-Americans living in Los Angeles and the county's low-income neighborhoods has decreased. Although U.S. government data rates many Los Angeles neighborhoods as poor, the proportion of their residents who have jobs has steadily increased.[10] Southern Californians have witnessed the creation of more work than at any time in the Los Angeles region's history, but the skewed distribution of wealth between high income and low income Angelenos (and this can be said for American workers as a whole) has also increased dramatically.

The extent of this inequality creates a tension which is necessary for community and economic organizing. It is this creative tension between change and harmony that leads to new possibilities.[11] The poor know the world as it is but they also imagine how it should be. Although the great majority of first generation immigrants might accept low pay, harsh working conditions, and an "okay" standard of living, we have multiple cases of undocumented workers who have organized and led campaigns for unionization. It is their children, however, who will surely become discontented without further opportunities for greater socioeconomic success. One organizes to insure that all participants in the work world obtain a living wage, and one also organizes to create economic development through job creation. Such organizing occurs across the United States today and will continue to occur into the future as long as exponential economic inequities exist.

At the end of the twentieth century a tsunami of Latino immigrants broke over the African-American population of Los Angeles, pushing this population into other Southern California counties—primarily Riverside and San Bernardino but also Ventura, Santa Ana, and Orange. On the one hand, a natural tension exists because many low-income African-Americans continue to face economic and social struggles of their own. The ongoing flow of immigrants puts further pressure on the local infrastructure. In addition, the Latino population is rapidly increasing in these once outlying areas of Los Angeles. On the other hand, African-American property owners have benefited from the Hispanic immigration to Southern California because the market value of their homes has gone up as well as residential rental rates. It is the proverbial mixed bag.

> Latinos are bringing redemptive energies to the neglected, worn-out cores and inner suburbs of many metropolitan areas. The process is most vivid in cities, especially in the Southwest, where immigrants have access to homeownership, even if that involves the leveraging of mortgages through the combination of three or even four low-wage adult incomes. A remarkable case is the

belt of old (circa 1920) bungalow neighborhoods directly south and southeast of downtown Los Angeles. Here, in the aftermath of the 1965 Watts riot, bank "redlining," civic indifference, and absentee landlordism accelerated the decay of an aging, poorly built housing stock. Yet today, even in the historically poorest census tracts, including most of the Central-Vernon, Florence-Firestone, and Watts-Willowbrook districts, there is not a street that has not been dramatically brightened by new immigrants. Tired, sad little homes undergo miraculous revivifications: their peeling facades repainted, sagging roofs and porches rebuilt and yellowing lawns replanted in cacti and azaleas. Cumulatively the sweat equity of 75,000 or so Mexican and Salvadorean homeowners has become an unexcelled constructive force (the opposite of white flight) working to restore debilitated neighborhoods to trim respectability. Moreover, the insatiable immigrant demand for family housing has allowed older African-American residents to reap unexpected gains in home sales: a serendipitous aspect of "ethnic succession" that has been ignored by analysts who focus only on the rough edges of black/Latino relations.[12]

The five county Los Angeles metropolitan population has grown twice as fast as the national average during the past fifteen years and more than sixteen million people now call metropolitan Los Angeles home. The racial/ethnic breakdown is 40 percent Latino, 39 percent white, 10 percent Asian, and 7 percent black. A third of the region's residents were born outside of the United States.[13] The Los Angeles region has seen its Hispanic population increase in the last thirty years, and the percentage of poor neighborhoods has similarly increased. Nationally the number of people in poor neighborhoods or very poor neighborhoods has declined.[14] Latinos constitute 65 percent of the inhabitants of very poor neighborhoods in the region.[15] While the educational level of these areas has decreased in the last thirty years, the rate of employment has increased. Poor and uneducated Latinos are taking any type of job to put tortillas on the table. The staffs of churches, community organizations, and labor unions that organize in these areas observe large numbers of working poor; in addition, these poor are predominately family households because the number of single parent families has decreased in low-income neighborhoods. Poor neighborhoods of Los Angeles include separately incorporated cities, and any native Angeleno will identify at least some of them when asked to point them out; e.g., East Los Angeles, Compton, Huntington Park (the community with the highest percentage of Mexican immigrants in the nation), Pico-Union, Bell Gardens, Maywood, and Vernon.

Chicago is the third largest city in the United States, the third largest metropolitan area, and the "gateway" city for Latinos in the Midwest. Cleveland, Columbus, Detroit, Indianapolis, Kansas City, and Minneapolis-St. Paul have all experienced increases in their Hispanic numbers but Chicago's has been exponential relative to the others. The 2000 census data reveals that over half of Chicago's foreign-born residents come from Mexico. In metropolitan Chicago, Mexicans make up 18.5 percent of the manufacturing workers, up from 6.1 percent in 1980.[16] This immigration process has rejuvenated neighborhoods in the southwest and northwest areas of the city. Demographic data, however, shows that many new arrivals settle in suburban areas and not simply the urban center, which also is true for other metropolitan areas. As of 2000, the annual income for blacks is $29,000, Hispanics $37,000, and whites $49,000. The Brookings Institute reports that many Chicago residents are working poor with incomes that are between 100 percent and 150 percent of the poverty level. Despite their low income, Hispanics comprise a steadily growing percentage of the homeowners in the city and their continued economic success is irrefutable. As early as the mid-1990s, the 26th Street corridor in the Little Village neighborhood had the highest sales tax revenue in the city.[17] Many more people in these communities have the desire and potential to follow their family and friends in upward mobility. Among twenty-three of the largest American cities, Chicago and Los Angeles have the largest size households (2.67 and 2.8 persons, respectively) and the most families that consist of married couples with children.[18] Hispanic culture, supported by Catholic culture, more often sees planned or unplanned children as welcomed family additions. One has a basic awareness that if new life cannot be accepted through children, then life is never fully respected at any stage.

Washington, D.C., is considered by U.S. demographers as an "emerging immigrant gateway city." A little over 51,000 of Washington's population of half-million are Latinos. Close to half (46.3 percent) of D.C. Latinos live in Ward 1 neighborhoods: Kalorama Heights/Adams Morgan/Lanier Heights, Mount Pleasant/Columbia Heights/Pleasant Plains/Park View, and Howard University/Cardozo/Shaw/Le Droit Park.[19] During the 1990s, Washington, D.C., lost population but its surrounding suburbs like many southern cities gained population. Hispanics live in Silver Spring/Langley Park, Md., Adams Morgan/Mount Pleasant, D.C., and Arlington/Fairfax, Va. While the suburbs saw an increase of 327,674 immigrants, Washington, D.C., itself only increased by 14,674 immigrants. In the metropolitan area, fully 30 percent of the immigrants were Latinos, with a significant number hailing from El Salvador. So the nation's capitol is becoming Hispanic too.

Will we see an Americanization of the Hispanic population or a Hispanification of the country? Los Angeles–based futurist Joel Kotkin argues that assimilation is already happening and that Latinos will follow a similar pattern to the Italians who within a generation or two lost their Italian language skills and became solidly middle class. Spanish language schools are nonexistent and interracial marriage makes race-sensitive, political-identity politicians appear stuck in a different time warp. In California, according to Kotkin, voter rejection of affirmative action at state colleges (Proposition 209) and bilingual education (Proposition 227) has marked a shift away from embracing identity politics that is not unwelcomed by some Latinos themselves.[20] Voters passed Proposition 209 with 54 percent of the vote. Asians, Hispanics, and African-Americans in fact rejected an end to affirmative action at state colleges by large margins while 54 percent of Roman Catholics supported it. Obviously, ethnicity is still important yet a desire for color blindness continues to influence the American psyche. Immigrant and native-born alike see the world as it is but know what it ought to be in theory. Exit polls reveal that more than one out of three Latino voters (37 percent) support an end to bilingual education, which is not an unsubstantial number.[21] A majority of union members (51 percent) and union households (57 percent) support the measure. In November 1997, 47 percent of the membership of the United Teachers of Los Angeles voted to support the English-only initiative, though their leadership urged them to oppose it.[22] Black voters opposed the initiative by a slim margin (52 percent) and the majority of Asian voters were supportive of English-only in public schools (57 percent). Voting non-Catholic Christians, Roman Catholics, and Jews all supported the initiative.[23] Immigrant rights activist Alice Callaghan has remarked that many monolingual, Spanish-speaking parents view bilingual education as an obstacle in their children's education and that none of the Mexican-American Legal Defense and Educational Fund (MALDEF) lawyers she knew had their children in bilingual education.[24]

In the case of Proposition 187 ("Save Our State": no public support of the undocumented), statistical analysis of the voting supported the conclusion that Californians who had voted for the initiative perceived immigrants as contributing to a poor economy in the early 1990s even when individual voters were personally in financially sound positions. The support of Proposition 187 harkens back to similar immigrant backlashes during economic downturns between 1929 and 1933 when Mexican immigrants and native-born Mexican-Americans were deported. It also goes back to the Operation Wetback period in the 1950s.[25] Unlike today's Minutemen activities at the border, the U.S. government officially repatriated over 250,000 Mexicans back to Mexico during the Depression and hundreds of thousands more during Operation Wetback. Many of the repatriated children were American-born.[26]

Thirty-three percent of the Latino voters also supported Proposition 187, although pundits had expected much more support from the Latino electorate. The Archdiocese of Los Angeles conducted a parish level effort to educate Catholics about the negative effects of Proposition 187 and what some described as its inherent "anti-immigrant meanness."[27] Exit polls revealed that 49 percent of the Catholics supported the proposition and 59 percent of the non-Hispanic Catholics voted for it. Los Angeles' Cardinal Roger Mahony bemoaned the poor formation of his Catholic flock, but surveys have consistently shown that large majorities of U.S. Catholics also support artificial contraception and legalized abortion despite Church teaching.[28] North American Catholics apparently respect their shepherds for spiritual guidance but, according to survey responses, do not always follow their lead on day-to-day moral decision making. Moreover, if Catholics are to even hear the Church views on a plethora of social concerns, they need to go to Mass. The Gallup Poll reported that, in 1965, 67 percent of the adult Catholics on any given week in the year attended Mass; by 2004 the number had dropped to 45 percent.[29]

Catholics in the United States, like the majority of U.S. citizens, want immigration tightened up, but the official Church has over time spoken much less about the right of countries to regulate their borders and limit immigration for the good of its present citizens. Biblical justice overrides ethical justice in the minds of some immigration supporters, but commentators remark that Church leaders sometimes forget that the Israelites were conscious and protective of their own borders as the Hebrew Testament attests:

Yahweh, remember what has happened to us; on us and see our degradation.
Our inheritance has passed to aliens, our homes to barbarians (Lamentations 5:2).

Sun and moon grow dark, the stars lose their brilliance.
Yahweh roars from Zion, makes his voice heard from Jerusalem;
heaven and earth tremble.
But Yahweh will be a shelter for his people, a stronghold for sons of Israel.
You will learn then that I am Yahweh your God, dwelling in Zion, my holy mountain.
Jerusalem will be a holy place,
no alien will ever pass through it again (Joel 4:16–17).[30]

Common sense suggests that limits and restrictions on immigration are neither uncompassionate nor unwarranted when a people feel besieged. Nonetheless, since scripture continually reminds us of our own exile, wanderings, and responsibility toward the sojourner, Christians must not allow the xenophobic hysteria of the few to become imprudent policies for the many. Scripture incontestably says "I tell you solemnly, in so far as you did this to one of the least of these brothers of mine, you did it to me." (Matthew 25:40) We are always our brother's keeper. The U.S. Conference of Catholic Bishops has just recently launched its campaign *Justice for Immigrants: A Journey of Hope* to educate Catholics of the benefits we receive from immigrants, to encourage a reasonable guest-worker program, to respond to anti-immigrant anger, and to promote family reunification. The issue will remain one of compassion and prudence.

During the immigration reform debates of the mid-1980s, both the MALDEF and the League of United Latin American Citizens (LULAC), two preeminent national Latino organizations, provided the vocal opposition to the Simpson-Mazzoli immigration legislation that ultimately became the Immigration Reform and Control Act which granted amnesty to illegal immigrants.[31] Latino politicians were also publicly opposed to the reform but more conflicted because they knew that Mexican-Americans were in fact divided over the issue. Mexican-Americans often wanted help for native-born residents first before taking care of new arrivals.[32]

Researchers have reported negative public-sector consequences due to immigration and have called for skills-selective, legal immigration of a moderate range, approximately 300,000 per year.[33] The bigger issue for American citizens is whether we can sacrifice some of our relatively high standard of living (that is, curb our appetites) to promote better education, health care, and work opportunities for literally millions of potential émigrés from around the world. As for Proposition 187, court battles began immediately over the denial of public health and education services to the undocumented, and within five years Governor Gray Davis saw it as unenforceable. Some commentators have also suggested that naturalizations, Latino voter registrations, and workplace organizing efforts went up in response to the victory of Proposition 187, the Save Our State initiative.[34]

What Does the U.S. Catholic Church Say about This Latino Population?

In 1986, the National Conference of Catholic Bishops published "Together a New People," a pastoral statement of migrants and immigrants. The document reasserts the Church's traditional position of welcoming the foreigner who finds himself in a foreign land. The Catholic Church in the United

States is historically an immigrant Church that encouraged the building of national parishes, relied on clergy from the homelands of immigrants, and defended the rights of immigrants in American society.[35]

> The pastoral letters of the U.S. Catholic bishops and the pastoral practices of dioceses and parishes document a tradition of welcome into the social church where there are no more distinctions between Jew and Greek, slave and free, male and female, but all are one in Christ Jesus (Galatians 3:28). A church of many nations, the Catholic community was called to develop an attitude of welcome, mindful of the Lord's words: "He who welcomes you welcomes me" (Matthew 10:40). It was challenged to reach out to the poor and the marginal and open ways to full participation, because when a stranger sojourns with you in your land, you shall not do him wrong . . . he shall be to you as the native among you, and you love him as yourself (Leviticus 19:33–34). At the same time, the presence of the immigrants made evident a living communion of churches throughout the world; the immigrants became a natural link with their countries of origin, advocates for their needs and bearers of new cultural expressions in the American mosaic.[36]

The bishops are well aware of the controversies surrounding immigration but consistently take a position of caring for the human being no matter his or her origin or legal status within the United States While recognizing the strains that immigrants can place on society, the bishops when speaking before Congress and making policy statements have always clearly stated that "the application of basic principles of human rights takes precedence over legal rights."[37] The work of the U.S. Catholic Church is service and evangelization. John Paul II exhorted Catholics and their institutions to become the model of integration of all people into our larger society. When parishes are united despite language and cultural differences, Catholics give testimony to their construction of a civilization of love. John Paul II wrote in his address to the World Congress on the pastoral care of immigrants (October 17, 1985): "Thanks to the Holy Spirit, they [Catholics] should work ceaselessly to build up a people of brothers, speaking the language of love, to be a ferment in the construction of human unity, a civilization of love."

The Catholic Church definitely has a vested interest in Latinos because 70.2 percent of them are at least nominally Catholics (twenty-five million people), and a full 93 percent self-identify as Christian (over thirty-four million people).[38] Each local parish, Catholic school or university has a responsibility to welcome new people, which means responding to their individual, familial, and communal needs. Many bishops, men and women religious, deacons, and their lay partners have taken the time to learn Spanish and participate in cultural immersion programs like those directed by the Mexican-American Cultural Center in San Antonio, Texas. Religious orders have organized pastoral teams for retreats and catechetical instruction; e.g., the Jesuits' Ignatius Institute of Spirituality in Southern California and the *Instituto Cultural de Lidereazago en El Medio-Oeste* based in Detroit, Michigan, a collaborative project with Jesuits in Mexico. Dioceses have established offices for Hispanic ministry. The U.S. Catholic Conference in Washington, D.C., has an Office of Immigration and Refugee Services, and the National Conference of Catholic Bishops has an ongoing Committee on Migration. The Catholic Church is attempting to welcome Latinos and meet their needs. It has had some success. In an earlier time, the Catholic Church served European immigrants in a similar fashion because they, too, felt isolated and experienced what sociologists call social deprivation. Through all of its institutions the Catholic community is putting into action the Eucharist celebration that draws disparate parts into one body. Communion is the celebrated sign of unity, and the pastoral care given to new arrivals and the skills and efforts given by them to the Catholic Church are a potent force of mutual sacrifice within our society. Catholic institutions are obligated to manifest the equality before God of all his sons and daughters.

This unity has mutual benefits because the Latino immigrant community has revitalized parishes by providing young families, adding new skills, linking parishes to other parts of the world, and producing leaders and vocations among other contributions. The long-term parishioners find caregivers, social and business opportunities, friends and spouses. They experience spiritual awakenings and devotional practices that affirm their faith. The immigrants find a community that provides local knowledge and support for them as they establish their families in a new land. The U.S. bishops encourage their priests and church communities to help new arrivals protect their cultural and individual identities. By serving one another, the new and the old become goods and experiences held in common, which is true communion. In one's personal faith journey, loving your neighbor as yourself is essential to the life well lived. Those immigrants who dream of returning to their homelands someday, according to the U.S. bishops, have a responsibility to their local host community as well. The relationship is reciprocal and mutual in its gifts.

The U.S. Catholic Church recognizes the importance of caring for immigrants who are elderly, sick, or too young to care for themselves. In addition, the Catholic leadership insists that our society protect the human rights of all people and, therefore, the undocumented. When they are sick, detained or in need of basic human needs—e.g., food and shelter—the Church must respond. Since they live an underground existence and are, therefore, voiceless, Church people are necessarily protectors of their rights. "While the government has a right to safeguard the common good by controlling immigration, an effort should be pursued to regularize as many undocumented immigrants as possible . . . in compassion and fairness, the Church reaches out to these multiple needs with its ministry of service and advocacy. A leaven in society, it promotes the rights of immigrants, migrants and refugees and protects them before local, state, and federal institutions."[39]

Immigration and Employment

Latino immigrants to the United States have less education than the native population, and they work in lower paying jobs. Less than 6 percent of the immigrants from Mexico, El Salvador, and Guatemala have a college education, and 60 percent do not have a high school diploma. On the whole, immigrants from Latin America have less education than immigrants coming from other parts of the world, and their disproportionate numbers in janitorial work, caregiving, and hospitality work evidence this reality. Over half of the total immigrant population in the United States speaks a language other than English at home, and a fifth of these new arrivals do not speak English well at all. Roughly 50 percent of the Latino immigrant population is speaking Spanish at home, but the great majority of intergenerational studies predict a loss of Spanish by the second or third generation. Author Nicolás Vaca states:

> For those who fear that Latinos will "Latinize" America into a mini-replica of their countries of origin and thus render it unrecognizable from the nation created by our Founding Fathers, there is enough evidence to suggest that such fears are unfounded. Latinos, it appears, are typical of your average run-of-the-mill immigrants who want little more than to prosper under the political, economic, and legal systems in America. The difference is that unlike their European counterparts who have stopped arriving on America's shores, Latino immigrants continue to arrive in ever-increasing numbers. So what appears to be reluctance to embrace "American society" and, in particular, its language, is an illusion. The Latino population is not static but represents a continuing replenishment from Mexico and South America.[40]

Immigrants have much lower incomes than those native-born but within the immigrant population the poverty rate for Hispanics (22 percent) is significantly higher than the rates for European immigrants (9 percent) and Asian immigrants (13 percent). All immigrants are moving into the suburbs in higher numbers than before; 45 percent live in the inner city, 5 percent are rural dwellers, and 50 percent live in suburbs where they find more employment opportunities.[41]

In the last few years, Californians have watched Latino immigrants find work in agriculture, hotels and motels, construction, and manufacturing. A high number of Hispanics work in California's construction industry where relatively few African-Americans and other minorities are found. While in other parts of the United States it is common to find African-Americans in hospitality work, retail trade, construction and other similar industries, this is not true for California. Moreover, there is no denying that immigrant Latino job seekers have affected the urban work world once heavily populated by African-Americans. While some academics once argued that low skills of urban workers did not match the job characteristics needed by suburban employers in a post-modern high tech world (meaning high unemployment for low-skilled urban blacks), we find that in fact huge numbers of poorly educated Latinos have found urban work where until not too recently employment researchers assumed none existed.[42] Some African-Americans and white Americans may feel locked out of employment to some degree.

Roger Waldinger and Michael I. Lichter provide a mixed analysis of the issue of jobs and race. On the one hand, they contend that in some cases Latino immigrants and African-Americans are not competing for the same jobs. Latino immigrants are much more likely to take work with lower pay, poorer working conditions, and no benefits because relative to the work in their home countries the U.S. work pays well and offers a better life. On the other hand, competition must exist because they find that the relationship is often tense between Latinos and African-Americans. "Given the exclusionary effects of immigrant networks, the general preference among employers for immigrant workers, and the long-standing aversion of white managers towards African-Americans, the latter appear to face some formidable barriers to employment."[43] Nicolás Vaca, *The Presumed Alliance: The Unspoken Conflict between Latinos and Blacks and What It Means for America*, observes, "The reality is that a divide exists between Blacks and Latinos that no amount of camouflage can hide. For each analysis that finds that Latinos and Blacks have a "natural" basis for mutual support because of a common history of suffering and oppression, there are others that find great antipathy between the two groups." He cites the work of political scientist David Sears at the University of California at Los Angeles whose research in Los Angeles shows that half of the surveyed Latinos believe they are in economic, political, and social conflict with blacks while two-thirds of the blacks have a similar response toward the Latino population.[44] Yet, we know that ethnic and racial divisions also existed in the 1930s and 1940s during the height of the labor organizing across the United States. Ethnic divisions and racial differences do not have to impede economic and community organizing.

Latinos continue to arrive in the United States because they are hungry for work. They make their way here because social networks are in place to give them the support they need to survive and hopefully prosper. The immigration is facilitated by "kith and kin" relationships that contain the necessary trust to know that someone will be there for them. Once an immigrant seed community establishes itself others will follow the immigrant path. The academics call this the social-network theory of immigration. With today's communication and transportation systems, everyone has a brother, sister, or cousin back home or in the host country that is well versed in the opportunities or lack of opportunities that individuals face.[45] Since jobs become less skilled over time in an economy led by profits generated by technological cost savings, low-skilled service jobs become available when the price is right, and they become opportunities for immigrants. Furthermore, America's two-income professional families and their employers want housecleaning, gardening, childcare, elderly care, and maintenance workers at a low cost. The creation of professional jobs in global centers like Los Angeles provides low-skill, low-income jobs. Pierrette Hondagneu-Sotelo explains in *Doméstica: Immigrant Workers Cleaning and Caring in the Shadows of Affluence* that not too long ago observers predicted that with appliances, fast-food restaurants, and dry cleaning, most domestic help in the United States would disappear. But domestic employment has actually increased.[46]

Employers in services industries and semi-skilled manufacturing see the movement of Latino workers into the United States as a reflection of the global economy. Waldinger and Litcher reported some of the responses of these employers:

> Rephrased in the language of our respondent, the disparities between *here* [the U.S.] and *there* [home country] made all the difference: "Where *they* come from, five dollars an hour, at home, is a lot of money to them, where five dollars *here* is nothing"; "From where *they* are coming, working for these wages— *they* think it is great; For *them*, the basics is a lot; for people raised *here*, it is not worth it." Or, as clarified by one of our more sophisticated furniture industry respondents,"—the "that" consisting of unskilled work at "six-to-seven-dollar rates"—"*they* consider this a very good opportunity."[47]

Both Latino immigrants and employers depend on networks, one to find jobs and the other to meet potential workers. Employers cannot know the capacity of a worker by a single interview, and membership in an ethnic community provides a proxy for desired skills in a worker.

"Under all values lies the hard cash," reads a famous text in political economy. The employers we [Waldinger and Litcher] interviewed had apparently read the same manual praising network recruitment because it was cheap: "It does not cost us a penny"; "It saves me having to spend money on ads"; "It's easy and quick." But their interest was not simply to forego an outlay of physical or personal capital; network recruitment seemed to furnish a large often satisfactory supply of labor—sometimes "an unlimited supply of people"—with little, occasionally no, managerial effort. Existing ties to incumbents provided almost instant access to a latent labor force outside the workplace. "All you gotta do is just *think* about hiring people and then next thing you know you've got several people from other departments saying 'Hey, I understand you're hiring, and I got a friend' or 'My husband's out of work' . . . they just come out of the woodwork. This happens even before the job's posted."[48]

Even jobs that are low-skilled require trainers and a building-up of competency, and this means that friends and/or relatives are prepared to help. If there is no cooperation from co-workers an immigrant is in difficult straits. In the case of communication, an English-only speaker will obviously have problems breaking into a heavily non-English speaking department. Furniture manufacturers in Los Angeles will often have Spanish-speaking woodworkers and African-American delivery drivers. The African-Americans normally have more education and they are able to interact with English-speaking clients. The skewed distribution of workers among jobs is not simply racial but practical from both the employers' and employees' views. Yet, the network in the immigrant community that assists new entrants into the workplace has both positive and negative characteristics. For instance, employees who bring relatives or friends to the employer have to worry about their own reputations. The potential worker has to meet certain qualifications and once in the workplace follow the norms and procedures established by the employer and her peers. The use of social connections, however, may sometimes create a dysfunctional worksite based on nepotism and favoritism. In some cases, workers will build enough power through communal bonds to organize against the employer, using language and social identity as leveraging tools. Some employers fear that hiring too many kin can lead to labor organizing. Finally, potentially good employees are excluded (i.e., academically speaking, through "exclusionary closure") from the work community because they are not given the same support as those who are members of the in-group.[49] The best organizers capitalize on these bonds.

Waldinger and Lichter found throughout their studies of immigration and the social organization of work in Los Angeles that oftentimes African-Americans like native-born whites were not applying for low-skilled work. Hospitality employers often remarked that they were totally dependent on immigrants for new employees.[50] The researchers concluded that while employers were sometimes adverse to hiring African-Americans, it was the fact that they were *American* not that they were blacks that caused them to hesitate in hiring them. *Immigrants* simply worked harder for less. They see employers as the cause of the squeeze on African-Americans and not the tsunami of immigration experienced in Los Angeles over the past decade.

In Los Angeles, the Anglo-European population, whites, continue to hold the cream of limited-skill jobs that provide good wages, benefits, and social status. Jobs in manufacturing and the construction industry are predominately occupied by American whites, and this phenomenon exists in trade union membership as well. Latinos have increased their participation in the construction trades because they take laborer jobs which require little skill and they will work for non-union employers.

> In effect, less educated blacks find themselves squeezed into a narrow and shrinking segment of the labor market where competence in basic skill—literacy, numeracy, and communication—is a must, and the rewards of the work are consistent with the expectations entertained by most native workers. Further up the job ladder, where demand for schooling is greater, the concentrations of white workers grow more dense; further down, immigrant densities grow; thus (as unemployment and labor force participation statistics continue to attest) many African-Americans are becoming squeezed out.[51]

The state of organizing in California is more vibrant than the organizing found in other parts of the country. California has gained union members over the last ten years albeit the density of union membership has not kept abreast of the increase in the number of jobs. In addition, the state has experienced job losses in industries—apparel, leather, textile, motion picture, and broadcasting—that have been organized labor strongholds. Kate Bronfenbrenner and Robert Hickey report in *The State of Organizing in California: Challenges and Possibilities* that California has the most diverse worker population in the nation. In the case of Latinos, the percentage of Latino workers went from 22 percent to 27 percent of all workers between 1997 and 2002. As of 2002, 15 percent of California's union members were Hispanic. As has been the case historically, union density is low in industries with large numbers of women and minorities: agriculture, finance (almost nil), retail and wholesale trade and most of the service industries.[52] California unions have had relatively good success with National Labor Relations Board (NLRB) elections. California held 10 percent of the NLRB elections in the United States from 1997 to 2002 with annual union win rates going from 53 to 58 percent, which is consistently higher than that found throughout the United States. During this six-year period, California unions added 61,714 members through these wins, which were won primarily in already union-leaning "hot shops" that tend to be small, under fifty employees. In labor organizing, unions find huge economies of scale and significant power gains when large units of workers are organized. It is better to organize groups of one thousand or five thousand employees than a number of small units.[53] Locals from two unions, the Teamsters and the Service Employees International Union (SEIU), were involved in 46 percent of all elections, and 45 percent of all workers organized under the NLRB election procedures between 1997 and 2002.[54]

Some members enter into their unions through non-NLRB processes, for example, card checks, voluntary recognition, public-sector elections, and organizing under the Railway Labor Act. These workers include home care workers, airline employees, and state and county employees. The hotel workers have been quite successful at using card checks where the employer verifies that employees have signed cards for union representation. The employer accepts the card check as a sign of support and, consequently, concedes to a collective bargaining relationship with employees. In sum, Bronfenbrenner and Robert Hickey estimate that between 1997 and 2002 over 209,000 workers organized in California without using the NLRB.

They also found that unions are normally organizing global companies or subsidiaries of global companies and that organizing wins most often occur with employers that are 100 percent located in the United States. Company mobility is a significant issue because employers will run away from union organizing. For this reason, service companies and public sector employers (e.g., hotels, restaurants, hospitals, and schools) are more vulnerable to organizing because they must necessarily remain close to their customers, patients, and clients. Win rates between 1997 and 2002 were 34 percent in mobile industries as opposed to 54 percent in immobile industries. Bronfenbrenner and Hickey also discovered that the probability of organizing employers increases the more women and minority employees are in a unit. The highest win rate of 82 percent occurred in units with 75 percent or more minority women. Non-Anglo workers are open to organizing and in fact *immigrant* non-Anglos are sympathetic to organizing. While a small number of the elections they surveyed between 1997 and 2002 had recent immigrant workers (8 percent), they found that with 25 percent or more immigrants in the bargaining unit, the union won 58 percent of the organizing drives.[55] The bottom line is Latino immigrants can be successfully organized.

Naturally employers used various anti-union tactics to sway their workers against supporting collective representation. For instance, the success rate of union organizing campaigns goes down when employers hire management consultants, conduct supervisor one-on-ones, circulate anti-union leaflets, make plant closing threats, discharge union supporters, and conduct captive audience meetings among other legal and illegal tactics. The more employer anti-union tools are used the less likely are workers going to support the union. Bronfenbrenner and Hickey offer strategies that will assist organizers in their attempts at organizing workers:

1. Adequate and appropriate staff and financial resources.
2. Strategic targeting and research.
3. Active and representative rank-and-file organizing committees.
4. Active participation of member volunteer organizers.
5. Person-to-person contact inside and outside the workplace.
6. Benchmarks and assessments to monitor union support and set thresholds for moving ahead with the campaign.
7. Issues that resonate in the workplace and in the community.
8. Creative, escalating internal pressure tactics involving members in the workplace.
9. Creative, escalating external pressure tactics involving members outside the workplace at local, national, and/or international levels.
10. Building for the first contract during the organizing campaign.[56]

Notes

1. Martha Gimenez, "Latino/Hispanic—Who Needs a Name? The Case Against a Standardized Terminology," *The International Journal of Health Services*, 19 (3), 1989, 557–71.

2. Roberto R. Ramirez and G. Patricia de la Cruz, "The Hispanic Population in the United States: March 2002," *Current Population Reports*, P20–S45, U.S. Census Bureau, Washington, D.C., 2003.

3. Ibid., 2.

4. Ibid., 2–3.

5. Ibid., 3–4.

6. Ibid., 5–6.

7. Shannon McConville and Paul Ong, *The Trajectory of Poor Neighborhoods in Southern California, 1970–2000* (Washington, D.C.: The Brookings Institution, 2003), 10.

8. Ibid., 1.

9. Shannon McConville and Paul Ong classify poverty neighborhoods in two ways: (1) poor neighborhoods have a minimum of 20 percent of their residents living below the U.S. census poverty line and (2) the very poor live in neighborhoods with over 40 percent living in poverty.

10. Ibid.

11. See Edward Chambers with Michael A. Cowan, *Roots for Radical Organizing for Power, Action, and Justice* (New York: Continuum, 2003), 21–43 for a full understanding of the individual and social dynamics that lead struggling communities to organize for change.

12. Mike Davis, *Magical Urbanism: Latinos Reinvent the U.S. City* (New York: Verso Press, 2001).

13. Ibid., 2.

14. Ibid., 5.

15. Ibid., 10.

16. Rob Paral, Timothy Ready, Sung Chun, and Wei Sun, "Latino Demographic Growth in Metropolitan Chicago," *Research Reports: A Series of Papers by the Institute for Latino Studies and Research Associates*, Notre Dame University, 2004, 2, 21.

17. Jennifer Halperin, "The Walking Giant: Hispanics are mobilizing politically and growing as an economic force in Illinois. The powers that be would be wise to take note," *Illinois Issues*, Dec. 1994 at http://www.lib.niu.edu/ipo/ii941224.htm (visited Feb. 24, 2005).

18. "Chicago in Focus: A Profile for Census 2000," *Living Cities: The National Community Development Initiative*, at http://www.brookings.edu/dybdocroot/es/urban/livingcities/chicago.pdf (visited Feb. 23, 2005).

19. "Latinos in the District of Columbia: Demographics," *Office of Latino Affairs*, at http://ola.dc.gov/ola/cwp/view,a,3,q,568739,olaNav, percent7C32535 percent7C.asp (visited Feb. 24, 2005).

20. Joel Kotkin, "Survey: California: Just like the rest of us, like other immigrants before them, Latinos can be assimilated," *The Economist*, Apr. 29, 2004, http://www.joelkotkin.com/Commentary/Economistpercent20Justpercent20likepercent20the percent20rest percent20of percent20us.htm (visited Mar. 2, 2005).

21. Gregory Rodriguez, "Speaking in Tongues," *New Democratics Online*, http://www.ndol.org/ndol_ci.cfm?kaid=127&subid=170&contentid=1568 (visited Mar. 7, 2005).

22. Jill Stewart, "Cheers and Hisses," *New Times*, Jan. 7, 1999, http://www.onenation.org/9901/010799b.html (visited Mar. 8, 2005) and Gregory Rodriguez, "English Lesson in California," *Nation*, Apr. 20, 1998, http://www.onenation.org/0498/042098b.html (visited Mar. 8, 2005).

23. "Briefing Session: English Language Acquisition and California's Proposition 227," *Los Angeles Times*/CNN exit poll Tuesday June 2, 1998, Los Angeles Times/CNN exit poll Tuesday Jun. 2, 1998. http://www.wested.org/policy/pubs/prop227/main.htm (visited Mar. 7, 2005).

24. Antonía Hernandez, *Dictionary of Hispanic Biography*, Gale, 1996, http://www. galeschools.com/womens_history/bio/hernandez_a.htm (visited on May 20, 2005).

25. R. Michael Alvarez and Tara L. Butterfield, "The Resurgence of Nativism in California? The Case of Proposition 187 and Illegal Immigration," Social Science Working Paper 1020, California Institute of Technology, Oct. 1997.

26. Peter Skerry, *Mexican Americans: The Ambivalent Minority* (Boston: Harvard University Press,1993), 23.

27. James Adams, "Proposition 187 Lessons," *ZMAGAZINE*, March 1995, http:// www.zmag.org/zmag/articles/mar95adams.htm (visited Mar. 7, 2005).

28. Cathy Lynn Grossman and Rick Hampson, "Pope's death spotlights chasm between Vatican, U.S. Church," *USA Today*, Apr. 6, 2005, report survey data from the Alan Guttmacher Institute that estimates 27 percent of U.S. women who had abortions in 2000 were Catholic and rate of Catholic women of childbearing age who had abortions was 22 per 1000 as opposed to 21 per 1000 for all women.

29. Gallup Poll, Center for Applied Research in the Apostolate, http://cara .georgetown.edu/bulletin/ (visited Apr. 22, 2005).

30. David Simcox, "The Pope's Visit: Is Mass Immigration a Moral Imperative?" *The Social Contract*, Winter 1995–1996, 1–2.

31. Peter Skerry, 116–17.

32. Ibid., 268.

33. "Turn of the Tide? Immigration (anti-immigrant sentiment in California)," *The Economist*, Sept. 27, 1997, 29.

34. Roger Waldinger and Michael I. Lichter, *How the Other Half Works: Immigration and the Social Organization of Labor* (Berkeley, Calif.: University of California Press, 2003), 231.

35. "Together a New People, Pastoral Statement on Migrants and Refugees," National Conference of Catholic Bishops, Nov. 8, 1986, 2.

36. Ibid., 2.

37. Ibid., 6.

38. Gastón Espinosa, Virgilio Elizondo, and Jesse Miranda, "Hispanic Churches in American Public Life: Summary of Findings," *Interim Reports*, 2003.2, 2nd ed., Mar. 2003, 14.

39. Ibid., 10.

40. Roger Waldinger and Michael I. Lichter, *How the Other Half Works: Immigration and the Social Organization of Labor* (Berkeley: University of California Press, 2003), 200. See Peter Skerry, *Mexican Americans: The Ambivalent Minority*, for a further confirmation of this assimilation. Skerry asks if Latino immigrants will assimilate in the classical immigrant style, better education, better jobs, etc., or if they will take on the mantle of race victims.

41. "Executive Summary Insert: 2002 Demographic Characteristics of Immigrants," Population Resource Center, http://www.prcdc.org/summaries/immigrationinsert02/immigrationinsert02.html (visited Mar. 9, 2005).

42. Waldinger and Lichter, 7.

43. Ibid., 20.

44. Nicolás Vaca, *The Presumed Alliance: The Unspoken Conflict between Latinos and Blacks and What It Means for America* (Berkeley: University of California Press, 2004), 186 and David Sears, *Final Report: Assessment of Interracial/Interethnic Conflict in Los Angeles*, UCLA Center for Study and Resolution of Interracial/Interethnic Conflict, Mar. 12, 2002, p. 3, http://www.sscnet.ucla.edu/issr/crisp/report51.pdf (visited Apr. 3, 2005).

45. Waldinger and Lichter, 84.

46. Pierrette Hondagneu-Sotelo, *Doméstica: Immigrant Workers Cleaning and Caring in the Shadows of Affluence* (Berkeley: University of California Press, 2001), 4.

47. Waldinger and Lichter, 161.

48. Ibid., 103.

49. Ibid., 100–19.

50. Ibid., 214–15.

51. Ibid., 216.

52. Kate Bronfenbrenner and Robert Hickey, *The State of Organizing in California: Challenges and Possibilities*, 2002, 9.

53. Ibid., 12.

54. Ibid., 18.

55. Ibid., 28.

56. Ibid., 29, 30–31.

CHAPTER TWO

∼

Catholicism and Worklife

Scripture

The Catholic faith can make a difference when approaching others to organize on the job because of the tradition's understanding of work. For the Hebrews, God's chosen people, going to work meant serving God. The covenant relationship required a trust in Yahweh, perseverance during difficult moments, and thankfulness for gifts received. Yahweh asked them to obey the commandments and live. Through the covenant the Israelites had land to work, the Sabbath to rest, times of feasting and opportunities for reconciliation, for instance, the jubilee year and the forgiveness of debt. In their relationship with God the Hebrews developed culture out of their cult, in other words, norms for living derived from ritual practices. Social order ensued because they worked as a nation to create wealth but always with a focus on God's law, not simply accumulating wealth for the sake of wealth.

Right from the start rest was important to the Hebrew understanding of work. Working conditions included reasonable workweeks, vacation time, holidays, and sick leave. If labor brought us the weekend, then Holy Scripture brought us Sunday. Every contributor to an enterprise and society-at-large needs rest because God also rests in his glory, which is the fullness of contemplation. If God rests, then those who are made in his image must necessarily rest. If we fail to set aside a time to worship God, we are allowing our own worries to turn work into a false god. Sundays for the Catholic offers a moment of repose and sacred space for a more focused turn to God.[1] It might be said that the worker becomes only a machine and loses his dignity as a son or daughter of God when he or she has no rest. Even slaves according to the Hebrew scripture were afforded a day of rest. Work is at the service of humanity but only because this service gives praise and thanksgiving to God.

At times of feasts and on the Sabbath, the Hebrews were to do no heavy work (see Numbers 29:1). If we are little less than the angels, then we expect to have moments of rest and prolonged times of contemplation of our source of being. As the psalmist says of human beings, "You have made him little less than the angels, and crowned him with glory and honor. You have given him rule over the works of your hands, putting all things under his feet" (Psalm 8:6). Anyone, man or woman, who works, in the home, outside, at a desk, with his hands or his mind, knows with some reflection that he is part of a larger design, and for the theist it is necessarily part of God's grand design. Our duty is to follow God's plan. How do individual workers and enterprises fulfill this plan? In today's post-industrial society being employed is an essential first step. Most people find meaning in work and to become unemployed is to lose that meaning, to be left out of God's design. The sequence of steps is first job creation that leads to economic development and then the accumulation of wealth for the absolute maximum number of citizens: job creation before wealth accumulation.

People of goodwill understand that work is not born of need, desires for consumption, or societal pressures but born of humanity's role in continuing creation under the guidance of its Creator. Toil in its negative connotation happens as a result of our unwillingness to trust in God, in other words, sinning. The focus is on the transcendent when engaging in the immanent. It is not out of necessity that we work but it is our exalted destiny to work. And our occupation, if it is a moral one, should not matter, but our character in doing what we do is essential. God continues to provide the rain, soil, and other resources that we require for our sustenance and pleasure: "As long as the earth shall last, seedtime and harvest, cold and heat, summer and winter, day and night, shall not cease" (Genesis 8:22). If work is our destiny, then laziness and slothfulness are truly affronts to God's love. As scripture says, "The man who is idle at work is blood-brother to the destroyer" (Proverbs 18:9). "The diligent hand will govern, but the slothful will be enslaved" (Proverbs 12:24). Holy Scripture respects the work and dedication of the poor while admonishing others to recognize the needs of the less fortunate.

> You shall not defraud a poor and needy hired servant, whether he be one of your own countrymen or one of the aliens who live in your communities. You shall pay him each day's wages before sundown on the day itself, since he is

poor and looks forward to them. Otherwise he will cry to the Lord against you, and you will be held guilty (Deuteronomy 24:14).

He who has compassion on the poor lends to the Lord, and He will repay him for his good deed (Proverbs 19:17).

The scripture never says that rich and poor will disappear from our midst but that we as Christians must act in certain ways—e.g., with compassion, whether we are rich or poor.

From the Old Testament we find that kings, prophets, and priests worked. King David herded sheep as a young man, and some Jewish rabbis (not all) worked at manual occupations in addition to their studies and teaching. The prophet Jeremiah was a farmer. While we cannot justify a romantic notion of the sublime intertwining of work and religious vocation for the Old Testament people, we need to capture their awareness that work, participating in creative and life sustaining acts, was a blessing—a source of hope and joy in their existence. The toil they experienced, a toil that is an inevitable aspect of human life, results from sinfulness. Simply put, greed, envy, or perhaps mindless consumption are the sins that fail to relieve the burden of toil that we still face. As long as we persist in our sinfulness, humanity will trod forward collectively carrying unnecessary anxiety, frustration, and pain.

While the creation story portrays the curse of childbirth, which we call labor, as the pain of women, Adam is cursed to eke out his living by tilling the soil.

Accursed be the soil because of you. With suffering shall you get your food from it, every day of your life. It shall yield you brambles and thistles, and you shall eat wild plants. With sweat on your brow shall you eat your bread, until you return to the soil, as you were taken from it. For dust you are and to dust you shall return (Genesis 3:17).

God calls humanity to both work and rest. Each activity properly lived in virtue brings us closer to God, who is love. If our activities are focused on God, we recognize God's blessings in their fruitfulness. Doing good work is more than efficiency and effectiveness because they are worthless characteristics if we fail to perform them in a religious-moral framework. Rather than pray as if everything depends on God and work as if everything depends on us, we should pray as if everything depends on us and work as if everything depends on God. This suggests a fervent prayer life because we recognize our dependency on God and a reasonable pace of activity (work and rest) because we know that God ultimately provides for each of us. We are not working toward a utopian ideal that is exclusively our own achievement. Consequently, a large dollop of trust is a requirement as we go about our daily work. Scripture reminds us that the Heavenly Father is constantly blessing us.

> You visit the earth and water it:
> by drenching its furrows, by leveling its ridges,
> by softening it with showers, by blessing the first-fruits.
> You crown the year with your bounty,
> abundance flows wherever you pass;
> the desert pastures overflow,
> the hillsides are wrapped in joy,
> the meadows are dressed in flocks,
> the valleys are clothed in wheat,
> what shouts of joy, what singing (Psalm 65:9–13).

> The blessing of Yahweh is what brings riches, to this hard toil has nothing to add (Proverbs 10:22).

While humanity is to receive blessings for following God's direction in working and resting as sons and daughters, we also experience the wrath of God when we steal (failing to work) and obtain worldly gain at the expense of others. "The livelihood won by the wicked is illusory, he who sows virtue reaps a solid reward" (Proverbs 11:18). "To oppress the poor is to insult his Creator, to be kind to the needy is to honor Him" (Proverbs 14:31). "To make a fortune with the help of a lying tongue, such the idle fantasy of those who look for death" (Proverbs 21:6).

Jesus Christ, God made man, offers a cosmic reversal to the status of work, particularly in the minds of the pagans of his time and perhaps the materialists and secularists of our own. We, if we are willing to acknowledge Jesus as Our Lord and Savior, have received the spiritual grace to see work in a different light, one that frees us from becoming overwhelmed because we mistakenly live life as a burden. The Israelites understood their creative relationship with God but continued to work under the burden of original sin. Christ reconciles humanity to the Creator, the Vine-Master, and we as God's workers have co-creative responsibilities. The cosmic reversal occurs when the Vine-Master becomes another worker, like the great majority of us (most especially the immigrant day laborers), and shows us what it means to serve the Vine-Master. Jesus takes on the role of obedient servant and throughout the Gospel, although he is God, humbles himself by serving others. Since we were incapable of saving ourselves from death and destruction, he modeled for us the life of a true son or daughter of God and then gave himself up so that we might have eternal life with the Master.

Jesus, whose lineage descended from King David, was royalty but he was known to his contemporaries as a carpenter and the son of a carpenter. He came from the lowly town called Nazareth. Mary, Joseph and the infant Jesus experienced oppression in their own country, and at one point King Herod's persecution of the newborn forced them to immigrate to Egypt. They were immigrants, too, and this resonates with Catholic immigrants around the world.[2] The family remained there until Herod's death. Back in Nazareth, Jesus was an apprentice to Joseph in the family's shop. Jesus watched his parents work and then for most of his adult life worked as a carpenter or more correctly a woodworker. He knew a day's work and the necessity of a day's pay and, therefore, could identify with the lowliest of laborers and servants. When he washed the feet of his disciples at the Last Supper, he performed the work reserved for slaves. His humility, as a hallmark of right living, became the path for his disciples although the apostles struggled with this virtue as do contemporary men and women who live in this era of conspicuous consumption. The apostles did not give up their occupations, nor are we necessarily asked by God to renounce any particular ethical trade or profession. They continued to fish for their livelihood as they learned from Jesus, and they remained fishermen when they spread his message. By responding to the Lord, the disciples heard "the word made flesh" and added the dignity of Christian disciple to the work they were already performing. Can we capture such a path of discipleship in our modern lives? Aren't Latino immigrants living out this discipleship in their own labor?

The Lord's message is that God's kingdom is at hand, and our number one priority is to respond to this message. While we fulfill our duties as parents, workers, and friends, we trust in God.

> That is why I am telling you not to worry about your life and what you are to eat, nor about your body and how you are to clothe it. Surely life means more than food, and the body more than clothing! Look at the birds in the sky. They do not sow or reap or gather into barns; yet your heavenly Father feeds them. Are you not worth much more than they are? Can any of you, for all his worrying, add one single cubit to this span of life? And why worry about clothing? Think of the flowers growing in the fields; they never have to work or spin; yet I assure you that not even Solomon in all his regalia was robed like one of these. Now if that is how God clothes the grass in the field which is there today and thrown into the furnace tomorrow, will he not much more look after you, you men of little faith? So do not worry; do not say, "What are we to eat? What are we to drink? How are we to be clothed?" It is the pagans

who set their hearts on all these things. Your heavenly Father knows you need them all. Set your hearts on his kingdom first, and on his righteousness, and all these other things will be given you as well. So do not worry about tomorrow: tomorrow will take care of itself. Each day has enough trouble of its own (Matthew 6:25–34).

Edwin G. Kaiser, CPPS, suggests that St. Paul the Apostle in his tent-maker trade represents a dedicated worker, a charitable companion, a humble professional, and a joyful promoter of the Gospel. He was also a sojourner. Paul did not wait for others to provide his sustenance, but he went out and earned his daily bread. "For you remember, brethren, our labor and toil. We worked night and day so as not to be a burden to any of you while we preached to you the gospel of God" (1 Thessalonians 2:9). Paul reminded his audiences that he and his co-workers toiled with their own hands to maintain themselves. Kaiser calls Paul's admonishment to either work or not eat "the great Christian Magna Carta of Work":

> In the name of the Lord Jesus Christ, we urge you, brothers, to keep away from any of the brothers who refuses to work or to live according to the tradition we passed on to you.
>
> You know how you are supposed to imitate us: now we were not idle when we were with you, nor did we ever have our meals at anyone's table without paying for them; no, we worked night and day, slaving and straining, so as not to be a burden on any of you. This was not because we had no right to be, but in order to make ourselves an example for you to follow.
>
> We gave you a rule when we were with you: not to let anyone have any food if he refused to do any work. Now we hear that there are some of you who are living in idleness, doing no work themselves but interfering with everyone else's. In the Lord Jesus Christ, we order and call on people of this kind to go on quietly working and earning the food they eat.
>
> My brothers, never grow tired of doing what is right. If anyone refuses to obey what I have written in this letter, take note of him and have nothing to do with him, so that he will feel that he is in the wrong; though you are not to regard him as an enemy but as a brother in need of correction (2 Thessalonians 6–15).

St. Paul told of his toil to those around him:

> I have never asked anyone for money or clothes; you know for yourselves that the work I did earned enough to meet my needs and those of my companions. I did this to show you that this is how we must exert ourselves to support the

weak, remembering the words of the Lord Jesus, who himself said, "There is more happiness in giving than receiving.

When he had finished speaking he knelt down with them all and prayed. By now they were all in tears; they put their arms around Paul's neck and kissed him; what saddened them most was his saying they would never see his face again. Then they escorted him to the ship (Acts 20:33–38).

In a time of slave holding, St. Paul preached for equality before God. Whether one was a master or slave, one's efforts were dedicated to Jesus Christ. No matter your occupation, role, or status as a person, your efforts had to focus on serving God or serving God through others. Work, even when it is sacrificial toil (think of the small and mundane activities that seem to fill many days, or relatively monotonous work, or the unfortunate hard physical labor of so many Latinos; e.g., farmworkers), should be seen as a loving and obedient response to God and not a grim subservient burden. "Let the message of Christ, in all its richness, find a home with you. Teach each other, and advise each other, in all wisdom. With gratitude in your hearts sing psalms and hymns and inspired songs to God; and never say or do anything [e.g., work] except in the name of the Lord Jesus, giving thanks to God the Father through him" (Colossians 3:17).

Finally, Paul reminds us that all disciples of Christ have a mission to share the good news with others and this is work, with successes and failures, moments of toil and times of great harvest. Catholics who evangelize, feed the poor, lobby for justice, organize their fellow workers, and teach children their faith are very much at work. Sowing the faith, reaping the harvest, building the Body of Christ in the world requires dedication, energy, and a trust in the Lord. Paul also believes that those who are hard at work in their religious outreach are worthy of some benefit. The shepherds cannot live without adequate wages:

Are Barnabas and I the only ones who are not allowed to stop working? Nobody ever planted a vineyard and refused to eat the fruit of it. Who has there ever been that kept a flock and did not feed on the milk from the flock? These may be only human comparisons, but does not the Law itself say the same thing? It is written in the Law of Moses: You must not put a muzzle on the ox when it is treading out the corn. Is it about oxen that God is concerned, or is there not an obvious reference to ourselves? Clearly this was written for our sake to show that the ploughman out to plough in expectation, and the thresher to thresh in the expectation of getting his share. If we have sown spiritual things for you, why should you be surprised if we harvest your material things? In fact we have never exercised this right. . . . Do you know what my reward is? It is this: in my preaching, to be able to offer the Good News free, and not insist on the rights which the gospel gives me (1 Corinthians 9:6–18).

St. Peter also teaches that while sustenance is necessary, pastoral leaders and leaders of any sort who have their followers at heart never make financial reward a priority in their jobs.

> Be the shepherds of the flock of God that is entrusted to you: watch over it, not simply as a duty but gladly, because God wants it; not for sordid money, but because you are eager to do it. Never be a dictator over any group that is put in your charge, but be an example that the whole flock can follow. When the chief shepherd appears, you will be given the crown of unfading glory (1 Peter 5:1–4).

Catholic writers have recognized work as a welcome part of our human condition and have attempted to refute cultures, such as the ancient Greeks, who denied the dignity of the work of everyman. According to the Genesis account, in Paradise God commanded that Adam and Eve cultivate the earth; work was a natural part of that existence: "Yahweh God took the man and settled him in the garden of Eden to cultivate and take care of it. Then Yahweh God gave the man this admonition. You may eat indeed of all the trees in the garden. Nevertheless of the tree of knowledge of good and evil you are not to eat, for on the day you eat of it you shall most surely die" (Genesis 2:16–17). Toiling for bread by the sweat of one's brow, because of original sin, superseded working and living in harmony with God's creation.

Our Church Fathers Acknowledge the Value of Work

The Fathers of the Church—Clement, Origen, Ambrose, Augustine—and others do not offer specific answers to immigration, economic development, and other work-related issues pertinent to the organizing of Catholic Latinos in the United States, but they speak of the charity, justice, and goodwill necessary for Christian living. The Christian tradition instructs us to help Hispanics and others by providing the means for them to help themselves (e.g., living wages). The Didache, or Teaching of the Twelve Apostles, which was written around 120 A.D., reminds its readers that the way of life is love of God and neighbor. It admonishes us to be people of charity:

> Do not hold your hands open for receiving and closed for giving. If you possess something by the labor of your hands, give it for the redemption of your sins. Do not be reluctant in giving, or murmur when you give, for you well know who He is who gives a good reward. Do not turn away from the needy, but

share all with your brother and do not claim that it is your own. For if you are sharers in immortal things, how much more in mortal.[3]

Clement of Alexandria reminded his readers to judge wisely when giving alms:

Alms are to be given, but with judgment, and to the deserving, that we may obtain a recompense from the Most High. But woe to those who have and who take under false pretenses, or who are able to help themselves and want to take from others. For he who has, and, to carry out false pretenses or out of laziness, takes, shall be condemned.[4]

Origen lifted up the cooperative and co-creative characteristics of work in the lives of every human being, with or without a person's personal acknowledgment of God:

God, wishing to exercise the human understanding in all countries (that it might not remain idle and unacquainted with the arts), created man a being full of wants, in order that by virtue of his very needy condition he might be compelled to be the inventor of arts, some of which minister to his subsistence, and others to his protection. For it was better that those who would not have sought out divine things, nor engaged in the study of philosophy, should be placed in a condition of want, in order that they might employ their understanding in the invention of the arts, than that they should altogether neglect the cultivation of their minds, because their condition was one of abundance. The want of the necessities of human life led to the invention on the one hand of the art of husbandry, on the other to that of the cultivation of the vine; again, to the art of gardening, and the arts of carpentry and smith work, by means of which were formed the tools required for the arts which ministers to the support of life. The want of covering, again, introduced the art of weaving, which followed that of wool-carding and spinning, and again, that of house building, and thus the intelligence of men ascended even to the art of architecture. The want of necessaries caused the products also of other places to be conveyed, by means of the arts of sailing and pilotage to those who were without.[5]

St. Ambrose composed a sermon on Joseph, the son of Jacob, whose brothers sold him into slavery to the Ishmaelites. They in turn sold him to one of the Egyptian Pharaoh's officials. Scripture says that God was with Joseph and his work always turned out well. Falsely accused of seducing his master's wife, he was jailed. Here too he excelled at his assignments and correctly interpreted two dreams. His talent and success eventually led the

Pharaoh to request dream interpretations from him, and Jacob, a slave, would become the viceroy to the Pharaoh.

> But as for what pertains to the moral interpretation, because our God wishes all men to be saved, through Joseph He also gave consolation to those who are in slavery, and He gave them instruction. Even in the lowliest status, men should learn that their character can be superior and that no state of life is devoid of virtue if the soul of the individual knows itself. The flesh is subject to slavery, not the spirit, and many humble servants are more free than their masters, if in their condition of slavery they consider that they should abstain from the works of a slave. Every sin is slavish, while blamelessness is free. . . . The man who makes his own masters is the slave to a wretched slavery indeed, for he wishes to have masters that he may fear; indeed nothing is so characteristic of slavery as the constant fear. But that man, whatever his servile status, will always be free who is not seduced by love or held by the chains of greed or bound by fear of reproach, who looks to the present with tranquility and is not afraid of the future. Doesn't it seem to you that a man of the latter kind is the master even in slavery, while one of the former kind is a slave even in liberty? Joseph was a slave, Pharaoh a ruler; the slavery of the one was happier than the sovereignty of the other. Indeed, all Egypt would have collapsed from famine unless Pharaoh had his sovereignty subject to the counsel of a mere servant.[6]

Latinos who work in the lowliest of occupations often show authentic happiness and thanks for gifts received even in what some might call a servile state. While injustices are always wrong, virtue is always right.

But St. Ambrose knew character alone did not feed a worker, and he writes in his commentary on Tobias:

> Give the hired servant his reward therefore and do not defraud him of the price of his labor, because you too are a hired servant of Christ, and He has sent you to His vineyard, and a heavenly reward is laid up for you. Do not therefore injure the servant working in truth nor the hired servant giving his life; do not despise the needy man who spends his life at his labor and maintains it by his hire. For this is to kill a man, to deny him the succor required for his life. You too are a hired servant on this earth; give his reward to the hired servant that you too may be able to say to the Lord when you pray: Give a reward to them that uphold thee.[7]

St. Augustine recounts that toil in human efforts was caused by the Fall. Yet the Christian finds joy in work because God's work in creation is brought to completion through the efforts of those made in his image. Through our faculty of reason and by our faith we too come to completion in our cooperation with and contemplation of God through work and prayer. We toil because sin is linked to temporal possessions while our true love is God, the eternal possession that all Christians and non-Christians seek. The earthly social distinctions between people are due to sin. Only through Christ is work dignified; despite burdens and frustration, the correct posture of the worker is praise and joy because the worker is following Christ to repose with the Father.[8] Working is a holy act because working is not for the accumulation of goods but the sharing of wealth. With such a perspective, hard work is linked to charity to those who are weak, poor, or occupied by spiritual labors on behalf of the community. St. Augustine highly esteems the myriad forms of labor—carpenters, builders, shoemakers, or any reputable occupation (not gambling or robbers, for instance)— because they all add to a social mortgage that is compiled in art, music, languages, and other human achievements.[9] Work in co-operation with God moves humanity along in its completeness.

The monastic rules of St. Basil and St. Benedict provided guides for *ora et labora*, prayer and work, that brought further respect to manual labor than had been given in non-Biblical communities. While the reading of scripture, contemplative prayer, and liturgy were principal moments in the monastic life, labor provided for the material needs of the community and became a source of charity for those in and around the monasteries. The monks became self-sufficient while simultaneously acknowledging their dependence on God, and they so occupied their daily lives that the attractions of the world became more remote to them. Wealthy men and women often gave up their earthly riches to take on slave-like tasks as monks and nuns in service to their community and the Church. Essentially, these religious offered themselves in charity to others. St. Benedict assigned times of prayer and work to his followers and organized them into roles to mimic the efficiency and industriousness of a hive of bees while growing in virtue. Historians have argued that monastic life saved western civilization from the decay of barbarianism wrought during the Middle Ages because monastic lives of virtue, study, and husbandry provided the social commitment and communal harmony necessary to bind Christian communities and maintain their faith. Men and women at-large could work more effectively, study more thoroughly, and contemplate God more deeply because monks have dedicated themselves to working for God and neighbor.

Pius XII in his encyclical on St. Benedict writes:

Besides, Venerable Brethren, the author and lawgiver of the Benedictine Order has another lesson for us, which is, indeed, freely and widely proclaimed today but far too often not properly reduced to practice as it should be. It is that human labor is not without dignity; is not a distasteful and burdensome thing, but rather something to be esteemed, an honor and a joy. A busy life, whether employed in the fields, in the profitable trades or in the liberal arts does not demean the mind but elevates it; does not reduce it to slavery but more truly gives it a certain mastery and power of direction over even the most difficult circumstances. Even Jesus, as a youth, still sheltered within the domestic walls, did not disdain to ply the carpenter's trade in his foster father's workshop; He wished to consecrate human toil with divine sweat. Let those therefore who labor in trades as well as those who are busy in the pursuit of literature and learning remember that they are performing a most noble task in winning their daily bread; they are not only providing for themselves and their best interests but can be of service to the entire community. Let them toil, as the Patriarch Benedict admonishes, with mind and soul elevated towards heaven, working not by force but through love; and a last word, even when they are defending their own legitimate rights, let them not be envious of the lot of others, labor not in disorder and tumult, but in tranquil and harmonious unity. Let them be mindful of those divine words "in the sweat of thy face shalt thou eat bread"; this law of obedience and expiation holds good for all men.[10]

Medieval Society

The medieval period consisted of stratified social roles, among them serf, freeman, and lord, and scriptural imagery linked them into an organic whole as the body of Christ. The hierarchy of the Church led the spiritual order and the kings and their vassals ruled the temporal. The various parts of the body recognized their purpose and function in the grand design of the Heavenly Father. Therefore, the end of each person and community was God's end as discerned by the Church. As in every social setting and age, questions of fairness and justice abounded but the underlying understanding recognized God as the arbiter and judge of all. The lives of all necessarily supported and advanced God's creation through the direction of the Church. The various classes had rights and responsibilities given their functions, and moral parameters relied on Christian teaching against greed, robbery, and the maltreatment of the poor and for fair wages and Christian love of neighbor.

Over the centuries European slave ownership ebbed as slaves became freemen and serfs. The number of freemen increased with time because towns and trade centers began to provide protection for asylum seekers. The medieval economy developed around trade, and relationships based on selling and buying as well as lending and borrowing became more prevalent. As Jesus said, the poor would always be with us, and the different segments of medieval society had distinct levels of wealth. When trading became more prevalent and monetary exchange a part of common life, Church teachings against the taking of interest became untenable. The community saw a gradual acceptance of interest payments although they were clearly never at the level of usury. Nonetheless, the Church rightly preached that salvation was the primary goal of men and women and, therefore, it condemned excessive profit-taking and inequitable exchanges between craft journeymen and their workingmen. St. Thomas argued that profit was necessary to sustain a country or home but profit for its account alone was sinful. Instead, our efforts required stipends for our sustenance or the common good. The Thomistic position was one of hard work for the glory of God and moderate living.[11] In similar fashion, medieval Church writers argued for the charging of just prices that did not exceed the value of the good being sold. The just price doctrine conforms to our understanding of supply and demand with variations in price depending on circumstances. As in the case of interest payments, pricing requires justification and should never approach price gouging. St. Thomas also argued that at times civil authorities could justifiably set prices for some goods. The point is always the common good and not the inordinate good for the few.[12] While theories of justice, rights, and duties existed in the medieval period, no one can deny the injustices, violence, and oppression that were common. No matter how you parceled the work and wealth, the serfs and slaves did the work and others grabbed the wealth. The first, second, and third harvests were divided so as to provide the minimum amount to sustain life for those at the bottom of the socioeconomic ladder and power and privilege to those at the top.

The guilds of the medieval period were religious in nature, celebrating religious feasts and engaging in acts of charity. They grew out of religious sensitivities to protect the economic well-being of their members, by caring for widows, orphans, and the ill, as well as providing daily sustenance for the strong. These were institutions that grew from below and not from the mandates of ecclesiastical or temporal powers. The guilds consisted of families in a common craft—fishmongers, bakers, shoemakers, knitters, and butchers—with workers categorized as masters, journeymen, and apprentices. The leader of the guild organized work, conducted business with buyers and sellers, and maintained order in the association. Merchant guilds also developed to promote and secure trade with other cities and nations.

Work had religious meaning for guild members. They highly valued quality products and services at just prices because of their moral standards. The guild distributed resources for work in an equitable manner and regulated pricing in the market to benefit all of its members. God's providence provided work and to have a trade was to have an honorable vocation. An industrious and pious craftsman had a role to play in the social system just as the monk, lord, or scholar. All of these roles and many others—soldier, farmer, and innkeeper—combined in an organic whole that linked the transcendent and the immanent. God was, is, and will be the God of heaven and the God of earth. A farmer did not labor just for himself but provided grain to the miller who supplied the baker who fed the merchant, the cobbler, and the laborer. Work was inextricably linked to the worship of God. Each man and woman had an assignment that was linked to another and, therefore, every person had dignity in his or her own right. Society depended on a basic level of respect for each other's vocation and as a result dignified work itself.

While taking centuries to dissolve, Reformation and Enlightenment thinking would weaken the medieval vision of governance and economic relationships. This led to advances in democracy, individual rights, laissez-faire views of commerce, the industrial revolution, capitalism, and today's globalization. Although the moral authority of early Church reformers and political activists remained grounded in a belief in God and Christian thought, over time (even given the vitality of religious belief in the United States), the linkage between one's work life and the work of God began to fade. In the twentieth century, many scholars argued that western civilization was passing into a post-Christian era. Today capitalism has become the overarching worldview. In the not too distant past, individuals and their enterprises worked to provide for their livelihood; now they work to accumulate capital, which is basically money. Since one's capacity to acquire goods or services, or the money to acquire them, is infinite, the seeking of wealth has no limits. The goal is profit maximization. Even if theft, lying, and other immoralities are still abhorred, the capitalist, the worker, and the citizen are immersed in a sea of profit-making and consumption, which wipes out a broader sense of organic social well-being. The sociologist Max Weber describes a "spirit of capitalism" as springing out of a Protestant understanding that rationalizes economic success as a sign of God's blessing. In other words, theoretically, living frugally and achieving economic prosperity reflects God's love for the prayerful and industrious Christian. In time, however, without recognition of the transcendent and fraternal concern for the less fortunate, the building of wealth begins to lose any religious justification; it becomes wealth for the sake of wealth. As Karl Marx suggested money becomes a fetish.

The entrepreneur and investors require resources for production and workers to produce the product. The owners of the means of production are dependent on their workers and the workers are dependent on the owners.

This argument can be made for service work as well. The great majority of workers in the United States sell their labor, if it has market value, for a price. Given that men and women are made in the image of God, the Catholic Church has preached consistently to encourage the repudiation of any view of human beings as a commodity. In fact, in the wake of the harshness of the industrial revolution, western societies, with significant support from vocal Christians, necessarily promoted labor laws, social benefits, and eventually a somewhat benign welfare-capitalism to protect workers from the harshness of a labor market that could easily provide less than a living wage. Society had quickly evolved from an organic whole to a division between workers and capital, and eventually to a society of multiple classes with a variety of interests. At the present time groups have organized around class, ethnicity, gender, and sexual orientation among other self-interests without a view of the larger whole. Clearly, the Church has never condemned profits or the free market because capitalism is a reasonable system for encouraging social development and providing goods and income. Owners, workers, and consumers can accept and justify this means of producing and distributing wealth, but only when the dignity of each human person is respected. While the utility of natural and human resources, economic self-interest, and the instrumental rationality of the production process (with increasingly effective and efficient production) are paramount to the capitalist system, the system must serve humanity, never humanity at the service of the system. The system becomes corrupted when capital creates wealth through the exploitation of human beings and creation. Catholics are duty bound to point out those occasions when the system no longer serves human beings. We, therefore, must make sure that the capitalist system doesn't exploit other human beings.

Briefly, Karl Marx repudiated capitalism because such an economic system ultimately alienated labor from the means of production and the resulting product. Ownership lied in the hands of the capitalist and the economic and social structure—government, church, and judicial system, for example—perpetuated the alienation experienced by the propertyless. Marx based his understanding of the division of classes and ultimate class warfare on dialectic materialism that denies the human person's spiritual being. For many religious-minded scholars, his analysis of the human experience fails because the material being of man cannot explain our human forms of consciousness. Spiritually minded thinkers would acknowledge our material nature. They would, however, argue that our transcendent nature, which Marx must necessarily deny, allows us to stand outside of nature and create phenomena like laws, government, and other social structures. This is clearly a much too brief reflection on Marxism and its strengths and weaknesses given its profound impact on social thinking in the nineteenth and twentieth centuries. The Church rejected Marxism outright because of its atheism although Catholic liberation theologians and others have used some Marxian thought for analysis of Third World economic and social conditions. In the United States, the Catholic Church has long preached the evils of atheistic communism to workers, and Catholic leaders have worked to prevent communist influence in American trade unions. Organized labor has also wisely eschewed a theoretical worldview that speaks of the inevitability of class war.[13]

Virtues and Work

Freedom—economic, political, and individual—comes with a cost. This cost entails *sacrifice* (times of labor, which are *sacred*) on the part of all people. As technological advances, government services, and production techniques have increased, men and women have been freed from many forms of toil, but labor is still necessary to continue technological advances, government activity, and all forms of production and services. Labor and the sacrifice it entails will always be a part of human existence. St. Thomas taught that all beings are actors, most assuredly God, because without action there is no being. As body and spirit we find ourselves in the temporal world, and we attempt to improve our lives, making ourselves complete in this world through our activities, most importantly our work. Work is a form of worship when we dedicate ourselves to perfection in our lives and the lives of our neighbors. We honor God, the Father of all. We have an infinite number of possibilities before us. Once the essential needs of life are met, we have the further capacity to transcend ourselves, truly living as the image of the Creator. Literature, art, science, research, music, sports, liturgical worship, and virtuous living similarly offer us the means of becoming more complete. As the positive elements made by others contribute to the progress of human history, our body and spirit hopefully become more significant in the direction and fulfillment of creation. Virtuous living (a moral life) is a transcendent quality of human nature that needs planting and nurturing in every moment. The act of working gives us one of those moments.

How might we think of work in today's world in light of globalization and the transnational movement of peoples, in particular the Latino immigrant population? Today we continue to cooperate in the work of the Creator when we engage our material world with a love for God and neighbor that constantly seeks justice. The creation story speaks of humanity having dominion over nature. Rightly understood it is a dominion that encourages us to use nature wisely for the benefit of all men and women and protecting it for future generations. Pius XI wrote in papal encyclical *Quadragesimo Anno* that God gave us the resources of the material world for our spiritual and material well-being. Therefore, the working of any person, immigrant or native-born, should be directed toward this goal. Working with God's nature for the perfection of God's creation, including us, is worshipping and honoring the Creator. Edwin Kaiser writes: "We rightly speak of the inalienable dignity of labor."[14] Each worker at once has a personal relationship with God in fulfilling his duties as a cooperative partner in ongoing creation and also a social relationship with those around him who support and benefit from his efforts. As Catholics, workers need to see the connection between their human achievement and the spiritual and material gifts God has bestowed upon them. Those who wish to improve the lives of people in material want, especially believers in God, ought to accept and encourage belief in the transcendent and the moral manifestation of this connection because a focus simply on material gains will ultimately lead them to failure and emptiness. Labor organizers need to see this more clearly when organizing Catholic Latinos. In other words, economic self-interest is not enough to organize workers and their managers in the long run. The most promising organizing route is one that promotes justice at the workplace and in the community so that each person recognizes the moral nature of his or her individual worklife and the justice nature of communal efforts. One does not simply labor for one's self, nor does one only labor for the other. The Christian understanding of labor is enveloped with charity, piety, and justice as one follows the will of God.

The Catholic moral impulse is to relieve the burdens of the weak and suffering in the world. Catholics are to aspire to bring their brothers and sisters up, not simply to achieve more in their own existence. As mentioned above, work will always be a part of human nature, but the goal is physically and spiritually healthy work that allows each person to see the spirit of God present in all of us. Christians know that Jesus carried his cross and that they can expect no less as they journey through this life. At the end of the nineteenth century, as the Industrial Revolution reached maturity and socialist thinkers promoted new forms of social cooperation, Pope Leo XIII reminded his flock in the encyclical *Rerum Novarum* that visions of a burdenless society were utopian and duped the very people they hoped to organize. Jesus was first a worker in his father's carpentry shop before he became a teacher. *The Word made Flesh in Christian belief necessarily means that work became sanctified when Jesus worked as a carpenter, God as man worked like us—by the sweat of his brow Jesus ate his bread.* Each worker shares in the sacrifice of Jesus Christ because Jesus Christ sacrificed himself for each one. Workers—employees, employers, managers, union and community organizers, political leaders, etc.—are following Jesus' lead and consequently growing in humanity by his cross and resurrection. Catholics believe that they make up the body of Christ in the world and that this body is united more than one day per week. When they extend out over the workforce during the week to complete tasks and activities as homemakers, caregivers, construction workers, service staff, street vendors, and jornaleros (day workers), their efforts are noble efforts when done out of love for Jesus Christ. So often in the Third World there are images of Jesus, Mary or perhaps Joseph in cabs and buses, on factory walls, and in humble homes. The efforts of the most common person in the most menial and mundane task is sanctified when completed for Christ. All actions in the world are in union with his actions when doing the will of the Father as he taught us to do. This requires discipline and faith to see through moments of hardship and failure. St. Paul reminds Christians to fight the good fight and not embrace hardship and burdens in a submissive way but to persevere. Jesus knew the criticisms and taunts of skeptics and cynics who failed to accept the intimate connection between his life and the will of God. His discipline in living righteously while facing the derision of others is a model for our lives.

There is a duty to work to provide for the needs of ourselves and others. There is also an obligation to work to establish healthy communities, and social cooperation is an inescapable characteristic of this effort. The need to work in order to sustain ourselves implies the right to work for all men and women. Today the United States public must call for jobs and wages for every potential worker that follow the civil rights path of equality in democracy springing from the 1960s and the hard organizing work of the 1930s and 1940s. Denying anyone the sustenance to live by denying him or her access to a job is an injustice. The Church also must promote fairness and a positive right to work that encourages education and training, political relationships, investment of capital, and protection of property. This is crucial to job creation. Civil rights are in fact vacuous without economic rights, and economic development requires adequate wages, sufficient benefits, and health and safety protections. Remember that Martin Luther King, Jr. was assassinated while supporting the economic demands of Memphis sanitation workers. He realized that civil rights and economic rights were the flip sides of the same coin. Every pope in the last 150 years has spoken for a society built around good work that provides for the well-being of the great majority of people who have less than adequate means to a livelihood and property throughout the world.[15]

To achieve these ends, Catholics are dependent on faith, hope, and love (what are called theological virtues). *Faith* trusts in the revelation of God in

nature and scripture, *hope* foresees an eternal life and will not give into de-
spair, and *love* essentially manifests the love of God in worship and the love
of one's neighbor. One's embracing of these virtues depends on grace, and
God provides the grace needed. Because of our supernatural acts, that is self-
transcendence, God supplies us with ever more grace and the grand gift of
virtuous living. The Catholic faithful should focus all their earthly efforts on
a love of God, and employers, workers, and labor organizers must at the minimum respect virtuous efforts.

Thomistic theologians underscore the cardinal virtues when considering
life or any element of life like work. For instance, prudence is the wisdom to
make decisions of conscience when faced with the exigencies of the world as
they really are. Being prudent means Catholics will live the Ten Commandments. In the work world prudence requires a humble acceptance of industrial relations and employee/employer rights. It requires thoughtfulness, con-
stancy, and diligence.[16] Justice, according to St. Thomas, is the habit of
giving to each person what is his or her right. Since justice pertains to both
the individual and the group, there are different forms of justice in Catholic
social thought. Commutative justice is the justice directed toward an individual, for example, in giving a good day's work to an employer and an employer fairly compensating the effort. This justice can also take place between groups of people or a single person in relationship to a group.
Distributive justice, a second form of justice, is the justice shown by the community to an individual in the proportionate distribution of the community's
various resources. The individual is within the group and is owed a share of
the fruits of the group. Justice in this case fails to occur when a society or
group provides less than sufficient housing, education, and income for members of a class or political identity within the entity. Distributive justice en-
compasses members within a community, and its vehicles are legislation,
courts, social service provisions, non-governmental mediating institutions
(e.g., churches and unions), and other communal means of distributing fairly
the costs and benefits found in any community.

Finally, the papal encyclicals of the twentieth century which call for a fair
distribution of the resources of creation have arisen from social justice and a
movement toward the common good in the Thomistic understanding of general justice. Extreme wealth and extreme poverty are unacceptable in a well-
ordered world. Wealth—abundant goods and services—is good, and the
wealth of individuals will vary, but excessive wealth in the midst of clear human need is sinful. Social justice focuses all of us on the common good of humanity in our positions as employers, employees, consumers, and producers.
While no local or global society will provide for the desires of all its members,

these societies should meet their members' basic needs. The Catholic must abhor greed, exploitation, and denial of each other in all its forms. Social charity, instead, arises from love that depends on justice that sets the right ordering of relations and resources in the world. A love for God drives this justice which in turn expresses a love for God's people. There are questions which need to be asked. Is there justice in the wage contracts offered workers in an employment-at-will work world? Are contracts fulfilled by both parties? Employers should pay living wages but wages and other human resource costs should not jeopardize the viability of the enterprise, whether it is privately or communally owned. The success of the organization requires a just balance between the meeting of needs of management, labor, and capital.[17] Pope Paul VI in his encyclical *Evangelii Nuntiandi* wrote:

> The Church considers it to be important to build up structures which are more human, more just, more respectful of the rights of the person and less oppressive and less enslaving, but she is conscious that the best structures and the most idealized system soon become inhuman if the inhuman inclinations of the human heart are not made wholesome, if those who live in these structures or who rule them do not undergo a conversion of heart and outlook.[18]

Conversions of the heart must lead to structural change. The 1971 Extraordinary Synod of Bishops speaks of the need to work for structural change in society:

> Action on behalf of justice and participation in the transformation of the world fully appear to us as a constitutive dimension of the preaching of the Gospel, or, in other words, of the Church's mission for the redemption of the human race and its liberation from every oppressive situation.[19]

The Catholic Bishops of the United States have also written in *The Hispanic Presence: Challenge and Commitment* (1984) and in the documents of the *Encuentro Nacional Hispano de Pastoral* for a transformation of U.S. society that will provide the opportunities and resources that Hispanics need to improve the lives of their families.[20] At the second *Encuentro Nacional* in 1977, priorities for Hispanics included evangelization, ministerial participation, human rights, integral education, political responsibility, and unity in pluralism. These priorities remain today.

The Gospel challenge and Catholic tradition are clear. Our joy and at times our burden is to work, and it is by our efforts we cooperate with God. We come closer to our maker in efforts that glorify Him through his creation. The Latino Catholic in the United States—citizen or non-citizen—participates in the inalienable dignity of labor just as every other man or woman. The common good of society requires that we increase the opportunities to work and give the laborer his due. Organized labor offers a proven means of promoting good work for God's sons and daughters. The following chapters will highlight the historical cooperation between labor and the Catholic Church to this end.

Notes

1. Edwin Kaiser, *Theology of Work* (Westminster, Md.: Newman Press, 1966), 49–50.

2. See Viriglio Elizondo, *Galilean Journey.*

3. Didache, *The Fathers of the Church* (New York: CIMA Publishing Co., Inc., 1947), Ch. 4, 1, 174.

4. Nicetas Bishop of Heraclea. From His Catena, *The Ante-Nicene Fathers*, II (Grand Rapids, Mich.: Wm. B. Eeerdmans Publishing Co., 1962), 578.

5. *Anti-Nicene Fathers II* (New York: Scribners, 1913), Bk. IV, c. LXXVI, 531 as quoted in Kaiser, *Theology of Work*, 1963.

6. St. Ambrose, Seven Exegetical Works, *The Fathers of the Church* (Washington, D.C.: The Catholic University of America Press, 1972), 65 (4.21), 202.

7. Louis Miles Zucker, *S. Ambrosii, De Tobia* (Washington, D.C.: The Catholic University of America Press, 1933), 103 (29), 91–93, as quoted in Edwin Kaiser, *Theology of Work*, 105.

8. Edwin Kaiser, *Theology of Work*, 108–12.

9. Ibid., 119.

10. Pope Pius XII, *Fulgens Radiatur*, 23 http://www.love2learn.net/educreader/encyclicals/piusxii/stbene.htm (visited Mar. 24, 2005).

11. Edwin Kaiser, *Theology of Work*, 172.

12. Ibid., 178.

13. See Donal Dorr, *Option for the Poor.* Dorr explains that the teaching of the magisterium thoughtfully shunned calls for revolution throughout the 1960s and 1970s that would have ended in massive bloodshed.

14. Ibid., 247.

15. Ibid., 260.

16. Ibid., 268.

17. Ibid., 285.

18. *Evangelii Nuntiandi*, No. 36.

19. "Justice in the World," Synod of Bishops Second General Assembly, Nov. 30, 1971, in *The Gospel of Peace and Justice*, 6, 514.

20. Allan Figueroa Deck, SJ, *The Second Wave: Hispanic Ministry and the Evangelization of Cultures* (New York: Paulist Press, 1989), 105.

CHAPTER THREE

~

U.S. Labor History and Catholic Participation

Organized Labor in the Early Nineteenth Century

The intent of chapters 3, 4, and 5 is primarily to provide an overview of labor history in the United States for those who are unacquainted with this history and to underscore key intersecting people and moments where the interests of organized labor and the Catholic Church converged. Large numbers of U.S. workers/immigrants have identified with the Catholic faith, and the Catholic Church has long advocated for the care of workers and immigrants. The Catholic Church steadfastly promotes the care of Latino immigrants and workers because of this tradition.

American employers have always sought cheap labor from abroad: indentured servants, slaves, and immigrants. The downtrodden, maligned, and mistreated inevitably seek justice. In the early 1800s American workers—artisans, mechanics, and laborers—some of whom had come as indentured servants to the United States, demanded shorter workweeks to gain more time to educate themselves and their children. This was not an inappropriate desire given that these workers were then enjoying a fuller participation in American political democracy. They longed to serve their families and each other in their present state and to build for the future not unlike the most recent Hispanic immigrants to America. They also organized for incomes beyond subsistence although the employers and cultural milieu of the time discouraged wages that could possibly lead to slothfulness and communal decadence. Early workingmen's councils and federations did not have the class consciousness of later worker associations or worker parties that formed after Karl Marx's writings and the expansion of capitalism; in other words, the division between labor and capital only became more marked in the late 1800s. The owner of a small shop, a journeyman, and perhaps apprentices were already facing competition from capitalists who sought larger markets and relied on cheaper labor (which is not unlike the impact of Wal-Mart in the retail industry today). The American aristocracy had attempted to deny craftsmen and artisans rights that American democracy upheld for all men, and the aggrieved workers as well as more common laborers organized to hold onto these rights. In fact, tanners, bricklayers, wharf workers, and similar craftspeople and laborers fought as patriots in the American Revolution.[1]

Work stoppages and protests occurred during the colonial period and after the Revolution. Philadelphia printers refused to work for less than six dollars per week in 1786. Shoemakers in Philadelphia struck for higher wages in 1806 but lost their protest when a trial judge ruled that they were a conspiracy against the public's well-being, a common-law ruling that threatened workers who sought to improve their lot collectively. The common workers, if not working out of clearly articulated religious principles, at least saw a basic right as producers to participate in the rewards of their efforts. The United States was a Protestant country, and the great influx of immigrant Catholics (mostly Irish and German) would come in waves at the middle and end of the nineteenth century. The success and failure of the journeymen societies they established paralleled the state of the economy. When the economy prospered, the workers had leverage on the employers; when the economy failed as it did more than once, the workers necessarily acquiesced to the unilateral demands of their employers.

While not widely known by Americans, prior to the rise of the industrial economy with its capitalist titans of the latter half of the nineteenth century, early labor theorists proposed the communal ownership of both the tools of production and the rewards gained from their common efforts. In one case, the Welsh industrialist and social reformer Robert Owen established the New Harmony commune in Indiana. Owen was a champion in his company and in other companies as well in Britain of fewer working hours, better working conditions, and education for the mill workers, who were often children. He traveled to the United States in 1824 and established the New Harmony Cooperative that combined communal living, schooling, manufacturing, and farming efforts that gave participants a say in their work lives. The cooperative was overrun with prospective members, faltered, and then failed because of the lack of philosophical and technical preparation. Owen had shared his views of production and the role of labor before Congress, and he would become the leader of a mass movement of trade unionists in Britain that created the Grand National Consolidated Trade Union. While his efforts did not lead to any new economic order, today's small, often Church supported cooperative efforts around the world can be traced back to his activities that planted the seeds of worker-ownership in the hearts and minds of social thinkers and their followers. The Catholic Church's Campaign for Human Development has provided seed money for numerous small cooperative ventures in the United States often benefiting Latino immigrants.

Workers and progressive writers in the United States and Europe argued that an association of workers/producers would serve the interests of working people, since developing capitalist economies and their employers could not assure them of a decent and relatively secure life as hired employees. People without resources listened to American labor advocates and social commentators like Horace Greeley, who promoted social utopianism along the lines of Charles Fourier, a Frenchman who believed workers could be linked by their natural God-given emotions such as a propensity for competition that could turn work into play. A community, what Fourier called a phalanx, would have 1,620 members that provided for their needs without suffering from the suffocation of thoughts and activities that one found in the specialization and instrumental rationality inherent to industrialization. When these cooperative associations failed, progressives established producer and consumer cooperatives but these, too, did not become widespread. The great majority of American workers were interested in achieving individual success and not joining theoretical communities. Catholic Church leaders in the United States also criticized Fourierism as being the "first step to socialism."[2] In the mid-1800s, George Henry Evans and other working people pressured politicians for land reform so that all Americans could own land, and their efforts led to the Homestead Act.[3] Workers were citizens looking for the well-being and respectability attained with property. They still saw themselves as family people and not as a working class subjugated by the capitalist class. In this vein, the ten-hour workday movement was not organized at the workplace but grew from political associations that focused on winning legislative fights for a shorter day. The assemblages that existed for these issues were reformist rather than revolutionary and not truly labor organizations formed to bargain with employers.

During the 1850s labor unions organized around skilled crafts and trades while the great masses of unskilled manual laborers were left unorganized. The trade unions fought to maintain closed shops, to protect wages, and decrease hours; creating a broad labor movement was not a concern.[4] Catholic immigrants formed immigrant aid societies to help new arrivals find employment and to better circumvent the social and economic obstacles of a new land. Catholic Irish formed the Irish Emigrant Aid Society in New York in 1841. In 1855, American Catholics of German descent established the German Catholic Central-Verein which they fashioned from the work of Bishop Wilhelm Emmanuel Von Ketteler who organized the German Catholic Congress of Mainz in 1848 to promote the role of common people in social governance. The Central-Verein created programs for life insurance, immigrant aid, and employment bureaus.[5] Social action became a more significant part of these organizations but it was not until the Church hierarchy made a more comprehensive pronouncement about the labor question that the Catholic faithful would know the Church stood with them in the new industrial world.

> However much Catholics singly or in groups might seek to uplift the working-man, there could be no meeting of the Church and organized labor until the hierarchy had seen fit to make some pertinent pronouncement. Before 1866 there was nothing definite said relating to labor unions except in so far as the American bishops had reflected the century-old concern of the Church about secret societies. This had begun with the constitution, *In eminenti*, of Pope Clement XII in 1738, which first condemned Freemasonry and prohibited Catholics from affiliating with it or aiding it in any way under penalty of excommunication from which they could be released only by the Holy See. Such fulminations against anti-social societies, or those which threatened injury to Church or State, were repeated and elaborated up until the time of Pope Leo XIII. That pontiff issued five encyclicals which attacked the Freemasons and kindred societies, and finally these condemnations were codified in three canons of the Code of Canon Law of 1918.[6]

At the same time, the U.S. Catholic hierarchy encouraged Catholics to strengthen their social bonds with non-Catholics and to perform their civic duties responsibly. The bishops wanted outstanding Catholic citizens to be the bulwark against anti-Catholicism.[7] The hierarchy's concerns, however, were the secrecy and socialism that could be found in the wider world of labor solidarity.[8] In 1866 at the Second Plenary Council of Baltimore (a meeting of American bishops), the bishops permitted Catholic membership in "workman associations" so long as they existed for the mutual benefit of workers and did not conspire against the Church or state.[9] Individual bishops at that time had distinct views of labor associations; for example, Bishop James Bayley of Newark condemned them while Archbishop John Lynch, the great Canadian friend of labor, applauded the exemption given to workers' associations that aided so many poor people.[10] Other bishops feared the intimidation that agitators might use in forcing fellow workers to became association supporters. The Catholic Church continued to uphold the right to private property and contract-at-will work agreements. By and large, the hierarchy took a cautious position on workers' associations out of fear of socialism and anti-Church views.

The Civil War would lead to an increase in trade unions as cities turned out more products and labor was in greater demand. At that time, labor newspapers like the *Working Man's Advocate* reappeared, and trade unions boycotted recalcitrant businesses out of labor solidarity. The advent of the national railroad system played a major role in national business expansion and contributed to the growth of gigantic corporations in steel, mining, and oil. The railroads often created Catholic centers because Irish immigrants helped build the railroads and worked on them. Cities like St. Paul, Omaha, St. Louis, and Spokane became Catholic islands in a Protestant sea, and Catholics began to organize in these railroad cities.

Terence Powderly, the second Grand Master Workman of the Knights of Labor and a Catholic, would later write about "the awakening" that occurred during and after the Civil War. Working people had come to see "life, liberty and the pursuit of happiness" as their rights because they had fought to abolish all forms of slavery in the land.

> "Life, liberty and the pursuit of happiness" are words that were being read and studied by the mechanics of the United States. Every time that these words were read they took on a deeper meaning. Liberty to live meant more than to be a slave to the whim or caprice of any man. The man who held ownership in his fellow-man had the right to so misuse that fellow-man as to deprive him of life, and, while the conditions of servitude were somewhat different between the white toiler of the North and his sable brother of the South, yet the result was the same when the master decided to use his power. Shutting off the supply of food from the black slave while holding him to the plantation was no worse than the discharge of the white mechanic and the sending the blacklist ahead of him when he left his home to seek for employment elsewhere.[11]

Once large scale industrial production made its appearance, it brought workers together, and labor activism began to stir in their communities. Since some companies had become national enterprises, labor groups had to develop links across the country to strengthen their economic position.[12] Once again disputes arose over the best means of promoting labor's ends. Some argued for craft unions, organized to extract from employers better wages and working conditions, while others supported reformist measures to promote political changes to improve the lot of all working people in general. A pattern developed around failures and successes. When employers broke strikes with private guards and government support, the call was for worker legislation. When labor parties and worker initiatives were defeated, the leadership turned to strict labor organizing and direct, local action.

In 1866, delegates from various local and national trade unions met to form the National Labor Union; it was a politically minded group and pushed for legislative reforms to improve the lives of all working people including seamstresses and African-Americans. The National Labor Union also called for the support of consumer and producer cooperatives and an eight-hour day. In part, the reformist bent of the leaders was a response to employer associations that had successfully defeated the concerted activities of their employees—political reform seemed to be the most feasible route to change.[13]

The National Labor Union moved through numerous reformist movements including the eight-hour day, the promotion of worker-owned cooperatives, and monetary reform. Employers circumvented eight-hour day statutes by promoting the passage of bills that permitted private employment agreements to supersede the eight-hour day laws, i.e., employers could make employment contracts that included workdays of more than eight hours per day. The worker cooperatives of the mid-century had now failed because of managerial ineptness, corruption, and worker-owner mistrust. In addition, the political calls for monetary reform in the United States were never fully understood by the great majority of workers.

The 1870s and 1880s would, however, mark a time of labor unrest, in part due to the industrial sector's vulnerability to work stoppages. Strikes occurred on the railroads and in the eastern anthracite coal mines in response to wage reductions and the general economic depression of the 1870s. New immigrants like the German Johann Most preached anarchism to foment the revolution of the working class. He was a proponent of revolution and class war.[14] The Molly Maguires, Irish Catholic miners in the East, engaged in terrorist activities, although these acts of violence had a direct relationship to the suppression of the coal miners' organizing activity by the coal companies.[15] Although labor radicalism was rejected by and large by a majority of laborers, employers around the nation responded to it with the use of Pinkerton agents and federal and state troops to quell labor unrest. The Chicago Haymarket Square bombing on May 4, 1886, occurring days after a one-day national strike for the eight-hour workday, sullied the reputation of the more pragmatic labor organizations and was instrumental in the downfall of the Knights of Labor, even though no Knights were involved. The Chicago criminal justice system ultimately tried and convicted innocent anarchist leaders as the instigators of the bombing. But revolutionary zeal found no home in American soil.

During the 1870s many Catholic bishops continued to use the Second Plenary documents of 1866 to give them freedom to speak on the labor question. On the one hand, the hierarchy in New Orleans affirmed the right of laboring people to join associations that had mutual benefit purposes. On the other hand, the bishops of Portland, Maine, and Rochester, New York, spoke out on the question of work in the industrial era[16]—against societies that were secret or that advocated doing wrong to individuals or classes in the society. The Catholic hierarchy had no common position on the social question. Meanwhile, penniless Catholic immigrants who continued to disembark in eastern ports found themselves facing the economic power of industrial capitalism that was hungry for cheap labor.

The Knights of Labor: Community and Labor

By 1872 the National Labor Union had collapsed from philosophical fights between those who wished to concentrate on trade union activities and those who called for legislative reforms. The National Labor Union, under the leadership of William Sylvis, had increasingly supported the development of cooperatives and political reforms but with little success. When the organization failed, it was supporting Greenbackism, a monetary reform that would have kept prices up and circulated more currency in the economy. Moreover, most labor leaders did not support calls for a labor party because they customarily produced votes for their favorite politicians in order to win their personal political favors.[17] Out of this ineffective and disappointing organizing mire rose the Knights of Labor.

The Holy Order of the Knights of Labor, whose goal was the betterment of all working men and women whether skilled or unskilled, was a milestone organization in U.S. labor history. In 1869, nine Philadelphian garment cutters reorganized themselves into the Knights of Labor after their Garment Cutters' Association dissolved. Unlike trade associations, the organization did not promote strikes and other concerted work actions. More militant members, however, pulled it into labor confrontations, and it supported strikes with some reservations when they did occur. Uriah Stephens, one of the original garment cutters and a former Baptist seminarian, argued for the organization in explicitly religious terms. He spoke of the universality of labor. Working people recognized the Knights because of the organization's rituals, and the members addressed the president as the Grand Master of Workmen. Stephens talked of all workmen being united without regard to nationality, race, or religion: "Creed, party and nationality are but outward garments and present no obstacle to the fusion of the hearts of worshipers of God, the Universal Father, and the workers for man, the universal brother."[18] Knights believed that enlightened working men and women could create a cooperative commonwealth that prevented inordinate inequalities in wealth, providing for all people in a just fashion. The second Grand Master Workman was Terence Powderly, a machinist of Irish Catholic background. By this time, workers in a multitude of trades participated in Knights' assemblies around the nation. Powderly convinced Cardinal James Gibbons of Baltimore of the organization's humanitarian positions, and the Cardinal similarly convinced Pope Leo XIII of the Knights' good intentions. In particular, the Knights' decision to make their internal activities more public helped their cause. The Church had remained concerned with secret fraternal organizations, like the anti-Catholic masons, and the same bishops and clergy had told Catholics not to join the Knights.

The Holy Order of the Knights of Labor grew out of artisan republicanism, a tradition that respected private property and virtuous living. The Order's republicanism, however, focused less on private property and more on citizenship which guaranteed basic rights to toilers—the rights to organize, to set union wages, and to work a reasonable number of hours.[19] The organization's rituals, social activities, and Judeo-Christian background made the Knights' organizers into veritable missionaries. They promoted a cooperative commonwealth of virtuous citizenry because virtue was seen as the antidote to the extreme self-interest found in a laissez-faire society.[20]

When the Knights first spread from Philadelphia into the iron and coal regions of western Pennsylvania, some Catholic priests had no qualms with their presence, as long as they met and discussed their issues openly. Other clerics, however, feared that the Knights might return to the clandestine and violent ways of the Molly Maguires. In 1878, Bishop William O'Hara of Scranton denied ever giving approval to Catholic membership in the Knights because he had not read the organization's bylaws. Jesuits and Redemptorist priests also preached against secret societies, including the Knights, during parish missions that were on par with Protestant revivals. Consequently, Catholic workers who wished to participate in the order were left to their own consciences. The Knights needed approval from the Church if they were to organize more Catholics. Terence Powderly argued against the oath-bound secrecy of the organization to assuage the fear of the Catholic prelates, and the General Assembly ultimately acquiesced in removing the oath in 1881.[21]

Similarly, the Grand Master Workman Powderly emphasized his political conservatism by criticizing the advocate of class revolution Johann Most because "Mr. Most does not in any way represent the views and aspirations of the workingmen of the United States" (Muscatine, *Weekly News*, June 23, 1883). When labor activists across the nation made preparations for the May 1, 1886 national strike for the eight-hour day, Powderly sent out a circular criticizing strikes and boycotts and advising against participation in the May 1 action. Powderly, in addition to being mayor of Scranton, Pennsylvania, was the co-owner of a tea shop. An extremely committed labor advocate, he was a charismatic speaker who led an exemplary life.[22] In part, his position against the May action was a message of conservatism to the Catholic Church as well.[23] The Knights District Assemblies were also notorious for initiating labor stoppages without sufficient support or strike funds. The Knights of Labor were a conservative group interested in communal prosperity and not class warfare.

> The Church has been watching our order for years. In our infancy we had but little power for good or for evil. Today we are the strongest as well as the weakest labor organization on earth. Strong in members and principles, strong in the justice of our demands if properly made, we are weak in the methods we use to set our claims before the world. Strikes are often the forerunners of lawless action. One blow brings another, and if a single act of ours encourages the anarchist element, we must meet the antagonism of the Church. I warn our members against hasty ill-considered action. The Church will not interfere with us so long as we maintain the law. If the law is wrong it is our duty to change it. I am ashamed to meet with clergymen and others to tell them that our order is composed of law-abiding, intelligent men, while the next dispatch brings news of some petty boycott or strike.[24]

The greatest opposition to the Knights of Labor came from Archbishop Elzear-Alexandre Taschereau of Quebec whose knowledge of the French Revolution surely played a role in his heightened suspicion when a secretive labor organization entered lower Canada. The Knights also had the misfortune of entering the Quebec area as Taschereau was investigating the Masons at the request of Rome.[25] He was the most critical Roman Catholic opponent of the Knights and sent out a circular forbidding Catholic participation once the Roman Congregation of Propaganda had condemned the Order in 1884 at his request.[26] Archbishop John Lynch of Toronto, however, was quite sympathetic toward the Order and argued that workers had the right to strike and organize boycotts against monopolies. Many U.S. bishops considered the condemnation letter received by Taschereau and the circular sent out by him as a local diocesan matter.

By 1886, there was much confusion in the North American Church over the status of the Knights because different dioceses had various views of the Order. In addition, labor turmoil was rampant. A railroad strike in St. Louis had virtually shut down the city for thirty days in 1885, and the strike leaders were Knights. Boycotts occurred in other regions of the country as well. The U.S. bishop's, however, were slow to act on Rome's order to the Archbishop of Quebec. Some U.S. bishops argued that Archbishop Taschereau's questions to Rome had set up the Knights of Labor for condemnation.[27] Archbishop Gibbons wrote that "masterly inactivity and a vigilant eye on [the Knight's] proceedings is the best thing to be done in the present junction" (Archives of the Archdiocese of Cincinnati, Gibbons to Bishop Elder, Baltimore, May 6, 1886). Archbishop Taschereau only acted for his local church according to Gibbons,[28] and Gibbons did not want to lose Catholic working men and women because of a poor understanding of the Knight's methods and goals.

In 1886, Cardinal Gibbons called a conference of U.S. Bishops and proposed that they discuss the nature of some of the labor associations and secret societies that had attracted many of the faithful. In October 1886, Powderly met with the bishops in Baltimore to explain the rules and activities of the Order. At the conclusion of the conference, the bishops condensed the notes of their discussions of the Knights of Labor and other "secret" organizations and sent them to Cardinal Simeoni in Rome. Cardinal Gibbons believed that a truly secret labor organization would result if Rome decided to condemn the Knights.[29] The memorandum sent to Rome explained why the Vatican should not consider the Knights a secret organization or a violent one. It commented that even President Grover Cleveland had accepted the necessity of the organization because workers had no protection from the civil government in their efforts for justice at the workplace. In early 1887, while Cardinal Gibbons visited Rome and met with Vatican officials in support of the Knights, the Congregation of Propaganda found no reason to condemn the Knights. Both Catholic and popular presses, even prior to the announcement, voiced the opinion that the American Catholic Church was on the side of labor.[30]

The Community Vision of the Knights of Labor

The Order stood out among other labor groups because its vision of the social economy was truly inclusive. All races, creeds, and ethnic groups of this period had members in the Knights of Labor.[31] A sense of universal brother-hood permeated the organization. It was a fraternal order, like others common to the era, and it grew as trade unionism was experiencing a decline. The members sought justification and support in Christianity, although they distanced themselves from reactionary clerics who they denounced for their "churchianity," a conservatism that valued a church's position within society rather than the promotion of gospel values.

Members learned workingman values from the Order's rituals and were often reprimanded for their vices such as drinking too much and failing to pay rent to their landlords. The General Assembly passed an amendment against liquor dealers in 1881: "No person who either sells or makes his living, or any part of it, by the sale of intoxicating drink, either as manufacturer, dealer or agent, or through any member of his family, can be admitted to membership in this order."[32] At the Philadelphia convention of the Knights of Labor in 1884, Powderly upbraided the convention for protesting the use of five cents of each member's monthly dues to establish a fund for striking or locked-out workers and pointed out the membership's wasteful intemperateness.

> We talk of reforming the world, why, we cannot reform ourselves! Do not look upon me as a fanatic or a radical upon this question of temperance, for I am not; I only ask that the men who are in the vanguard of reform, men who would accomplish something of benefit for the race, to stop for one moment now and ask whether we should not go a step further than others are willing to go in this direction. . . . When I meet a man whose reason has been drowned in drink, and look upon his face, I feel that I am looking upon a murderer, I am looking upon a person who has no regard for virtue or morality, for that which upholds virtue and sustains morality is lacking, the God-like gift of reason; incapable of judging whether his next step will be for good or evil, he plunges madly ahead and takes the dagger with a willing hand from his worst enemy only to plunge it to the heart of his most cherished friend.[33]

Similarly, a sense of chivalry ran through the group, and solidarity reinforced by elaborate ritual became a hallmark. Samuel Gompers, the first president of the American Federation of Labor (AFL), had been a Knight and to his death he kept the secrecy of the Order's rituals and signs as a matter of honor. This was clearly a social movement that saw men and women as free agents who were capable of living lives of virtue.[34]

Like the wealthy of the time, working men and women in this era believed in the nobility of human beings. They strived for moral perfection and held their peers accountable for transgressing the Knights' ethical codes.[35] Analytical studies of the development of the Knights of Labor assemblies in New

Jersey during the 1880s point to greater efforts and success in the community-wide organizing goal of building community solidarity rather than straightforward trade or industrial organizing. The goal was building an industrial commonwealth that included small businesses and worker-ownership. Mobilization was conclusively around the entire community, not simply the job site.[36]

Workers in one factory or industry were often not strong enough to force concessions or union recognition, except with the help of a community-wide boycott. They also prevented the housing and feeding of strikebreakers by enlisting the aid of shopkeepers. In addition, they could hope to win over local public opinion and to ostracize factory owners whose local authority, as sociologist Herbert Gutman has pointed out, was not yet legitimated. This tactic, of course, not only highlighted the importance of community-based organization, but it made organizing workers outside the industry just as important as inside it.[37]

In 1886, the Knights of Labor had grown to a significant size with 5,892 assemblies and 700,000 members.[38] Yet just as power was gained, it was lost by well-intentioned but poorly planned walkouts on robber baron Jay Gould's Southwest railroad system. Pinkerton employer-agents and government troops squelched a semi-supported grievance strike, and other employers took their cue from Gould's success.

Terence Powderly who sought to prevent strikes, but supported them when called, had responded to calls from fellow Knights for the development of worker cooperatives, and at one time the Knights had over 135 cooperatives,[39] including a coal mine in Indiana.[40] The majority of members, however, were more inclined to fight for immediate gains to be won from their employers. As a case in point, many Knights struck with other workers for the eight-hour day on May 1, 1886 over Powderly's objections. The Haymarket riot on May 4th in Chicago led to the death of both police and workers. Although not a Knights' event, it contributed to the downfall of the Knights because of the public's fear of anarchy.[41]

When Powderly and the Knights leadership turned to more abstract visions (a cooperative commonwealth), they lost the interest and drive of their memberships who focused on their immediate self-interests. Although the preamble of the Knights of Labor advocated for the development of producer and consumer cooperatives, the cooperativists failed miserably in their worker-ownership efforts, and few workers would contribute to the voluntary "Cooperation Fund."[42]

Kim Voss conducted a detailed analysis of the demise of the Knights of Labor in New Jersey and suggests that one might generalize her findings to other parts of the nation.[43] She believes that the Knights disappeared because of the rapid organization of employer associations and the money power of the employers. Comparative studies reveal that British employers made no such efforts because they had a more tolerant view of organized workforces, and French employers were slow to respond at this time because they had little financial resources to put up a fight.[44] In addition, while the state in France intervened in labor disputes on the behalf of workers, no such effort was made by the government in the United States; in fact, the government normally stayed out of labor disputes and only intervened to quell strikes on behalf of employers.[45] For this reason in part, organized labor to this day has played a more integral role in European economies than organized labor in the United States.

Trade Union Organizing: Pure and Simple Business Unions

The American Federation of Labor (AFL) would be the labor group that survived business's struggle to be free of organized workforces. During the 1890s, the AFL succeeded the Knights of Labor as the leading labor force in the United States. Adolph Strasser and Samuel Gompers were the no-nonsense leaders who promoted business unionism, and Gompers would lead trade unions into the future AFL. They explicitly argued that labor organizations had to make themselves more business-like and more focused on immediate membership concerns if they were to survive. This meant strict regulations, significant dues payments, union benefits, and sound business practices. The international trade unions and the AFL structures were more hierarchical than the Knights of Labor and, therefore, no local group had the power to call a strike, as often happened in Knights' assemblies, without approval from the international organization. Furthermore, the AFL was not promoting the organization of all workers, especially not the unskilled, nor advocating the creation of a workers' utopian commonwealth through cooperative efforts. Strasser and Gompers became the leaders of this federation movement because of their success in making the Cigar Makers International Union a viable labor organization. The death and strike benefits of the Cigar Makers International Union helped it reach a level of stability not known by more radical, class-conscious labor groups.[46] They acknowledged the views of their socialist and more anarchistic contemporaries, but they also saw the dissension and failure that occurred when working people moved away from what they called pure and simple unionism. Workers wanted to fight for immediate gains not farfetched utopias.[47] John L. Lewis, future president of the United Mine Workers of America (UMWA), learned this truth from Gompers, and Saul Alinsky, the father of community organizing, would similarly recognize the conservatism and traditionalism found in American culture. The opportunistic bargaining perspective of Gompers did help trade unions to survive and grow, but the lack of a broad-based agenda never pushed the trade unions to the even greater political and economic power they might have achieved. Gompers was not concerned about workers possessing the means of production. He just wanted more for them. Sixty years later, John L. Lewis, riding on the organizing drives spurred on by the New Deal, would attempt to achieve this greater level of power, but the backlash of the business interests once again would stifle further gains with the passage of the anti-labor Taft-Hartley Act in 1947.

Samuel Gompers, although himself a one-time member of the Knights of Labor, aligned himself with other national trade unions against what they thought was the Order's failure to adequately represent skilled workers. Gompers and the almost defunct Federation of Organized Trades and Labor Unions (organized in 1881) demanded that the Knights of Labor promote their pure and simple agenda over that of the assemblies of unskilled workers and refrain from interfering in national union disputes. When the Knights of Labor failed to take this tack, the AFL was organized at a Columbus, Ohio, meeting in December 1886. Gompers became the first AFL president.[48] The conservatism of Gompers ultimately won out. More radical unionists have called him a class collaborator.[49] We know that he was not a religious man, albeit a descendent of rabbis, and also quite a heavy drinker.[50] Terence Powderly called him and the AFL leadership "damn gin guzzling, potbellied, red nosed, scab faced, dirty shirted, unwashed, leather assed empty headed, two-faced, rattle headed, itch palmed scavengers in the field of labor reform."[51] The AFL leaders were not missionary labor unionists with the ideals of a moralist. Gompers trusted the abilities of the workingmen to win their own independence from oppression, and he paid little attention to intellectuals, populists, or other freethinkers.[52] As the AFL developed under Gompers, it became hierarchical and bureaucratic with Gompers as the head administrator. This bureaucraticization ended any social movement quality to the organizing work of the craft unions.

A second significant wave of Catholic immigration to the United States came during the 1890s. Sociologists Roger Finke and Rodney Stark contend that these immigrants, often Irish and German, encountered an aggressive clergy who promoted an "otherworldly" religion, devotional activities, and ethnic identity. The clergy worked with missionary zeal to create a Catholic revival that struggled to beat more established Protestant denominations in the religious market of saving souls. The Jesuits, Paulists, and Redemptorists had to work with evangelical fervor because the U.S.

government provided no subsidies to the Church as did its European counterparts. Parish missions and Catholic revival meetings revitalized the faith of the new arrivals. Finke and Stark describe well-planned one and two-week missions that the clergy conducted with business-like skillfulness to evangelize the Catholic immigrants.[53]

During the labor unrest of the 1890s and the growth of populism that unified both laborers and farmers, the AFL as an organization would stay out of party politics but continue to lobby for the end of child labor, the end of injunctions against labor unions, and the enactment of other legislation favorable to free trade unionism. In the first decade of the twentieth century as the wave of Catholic Italians reached America's shores, employers and workers took a more conciliatory approach to labor disagreements, especially after the volatile confrontations during the 1890s (notably the Homestead steel and Pullman railroad car strikes). The industrial titans at the beginning of the century (Mark Hanna, John Rockefeller, and others) worked with Samuel Gompers and other like-minded labor leaders as members of the National Civic Federation. This group acknowledged the existence of labor organizations and offered to help employers and these organizations reach mutually satisfying agreements. President Teddy Roosevelt would give support to coal miners when he called for arbitration with mine operators rather than simply ordering federal troops to quell the anthracite coal disputes in 1902.[54]

On the one hand, cooperation occurred because employers feared that too harsh a stance against labor would raise allegations of unlawful corporate trusts. On the other hand, labor, particularly Gompers, felt it was easier to bargain with an organized industry. Meanwhile, the Marxists and socialists accepted trusts as a natural development in the evolution of capitalism and its eventual demise.[55] This period of relative cooperation would not last long because union membership began to swell with more than a million workers joining unions between 1902 and 1904.[56] Employers once again insisted on yellow-dog contracts (employer/employee agreements where the employee gave up his or her right to unionize), sought injunctions to end concerted activity, and campaigned against closed shops and socialism.[57] Employers also formed the Citizens' Industrial Association and the National Association of Manufacturers to fight for the open shop, contending that individual freedom was lost when labor groups enforced closed union shops.

Yet despite the renewed legal and social threats against labor, Gompers and the AFL held close to their conservative path and refused to promote more radical or socialist answers to workers' woes. As a result of labor's unfavorable position vis-à-vis employers, the union movement began to lobby for legislative support to prevent the use of injunctions, yellow-dog contracts, and other such tactics to prevent organizing activity. At the same time, some state legislatures were passing minimum wage laws, worker compensation provisions, and child labor laws. Gomper's position held firm: he supported legislation that protected men and women but did not want government interference with wage and hour standards.[58] He believed unions could take care of their members.

During the progressive era (1890 to 1920), an era of fiscal and labor reform, President Woodrow Wilson aided labor's cause by supporting the Clayton Act of 1914. Although it was designed to prevent the use of injunctions against unions, various loopholes nullified its intent; it did, however, concede that labor was not a commodity and therefore not subject to antitrust laws. It also acknowledged the inappropriateness of the contract-at-will formula for industrial workers. But the Supreme Court would rule in 1937 that the liberty of employment-at-will contracts in our industrial society was a fiction.[59] Until 1914, employers had invoked the fourteenth amendment to the constitution as a means to prevent government regulation of contracts between companies and employees, that is, not requiring employers to recognize unions as bargaining representatives. "No State shall make or enforce any law which shall abridge the privileges or immunities of citizens of the United States; Nor shall any State deprive any person of life, liberty, or property, without due process of law; nor deny any person within its jurisdiction the equal protection of the laws." Although Congress wrote the fourteenth amendment for freed slaves, corporations (considered persons under the law) have long used it to protect corporate property rights.[60] Employment-at-will thinking to this day does not accept the right of employees to strengthen their position by bargaining as an organized group. Despite the development of labor relations and labor law, many managers still argue that employees cannot be truly free if they are not allowed to enter into individual agreements, that is, contract-at-will accords. The right to bargain collectively has been won and lost over the past sixty years because of this questionable position—questionable because a single worker cannot change the policies and procedures of a corporate employer and for this reason employees at times need collective power to find some balance in the employee-employer relationship. The Catholic Church has consistently argued in favor of the free association of people, including workers, since Leo XIII wrote *Rerum Novarum* in 1891. The Church was aware of the dangers of associations that condemned religion, but did not deny the importance of association.

> Certainly, the number of associations of almost every possible kind, especially of associations of workers, is now far greater than ever before. This is not the

place to inquire whence many of them originate, what object they have, or how they proceed. But the opinion is, and it is one confirmed by a good deal of evidence, that they are largely under the control of secret leaders and that these leaders apply principles which are in harmony with neither Christianity nor the welfare of States, and that, after having possession of all available work, they contrive that those who refuse to join with them will be forced by want to pay the penalty. Under these circumstances, workers who are Christians must choose one of two things; either to join associations in which it is greatly to be feared that there is danger to religion, or to form their own associations and unite their forces in such a way that they may be able manfully to free themselves from such unjust and intolerable oppression. Can they who refuse to place man's highest good in imminent jeopardy hesitate to affirm that the second course is by all means to be followed? (*Rerum Novarum* 1891, #74).

Union Movement Growth in the First Quarter of the Twentieth Century

Union membership continued to grow during the first quarter of the twentieth century. The United Mine Workers (in essence an industrial union within the AFL) became the biggest union in the country. The garment workers formed various unions—the International Ladies' Garment Workers, the United Garment Workers, and the Amalgamated Clothing Workers. However, it was the Industrial Workers of the World (IWW), the wobblies, who agitated and struck for the thousands of immigrant, unskilled, and disenfranchised workers—miners, lumberjacks, and textile workers. The owners of mines and logging operations employed thousands of people, and this work now required extensive capital for railroads, equipment, and smelting. The Rockefellers bought up Montana mining rights, and the Phelps Dodge Corporation became dominant in Arizona.[61] The IWW preached class warfare, although this was more rhetoric than substance, and conducted some extremely disciplined labor actions like the Lawrence, Massachusetts textile strike of 1912.

The founders of the IWW included Father T. J. Hagerty, a Catholic priest, Big Bill Haywood, and Mother Jones. They were nationally known labor radicals who organized and animated thousands of low-wage and low-skilled workers. While Father Hagerty saw no incongruity between his Roman Catholicism and Marxist rhetoric, the Catholic hierarchy would relieve him of his priestly duties, and in a short time he drifted away from labor activism and the priesthood. During the Lawrence textile strike, Catholic priests in Lawrence published condemnations of the wobblies for misleading immigrants, called for the end of the strike to the dismay of the strikers, and warned that civil unrest would lead the participants to damnation.[62] Cardinal William O'Connell of Boston sent Monsignor Michael Splaine, his chancellor, to mediate the dispute after receiving a request for help from Governor Eugene N. Foss. Monsignor Splaine's work with employers and workers proved successful when the priest helped bring a settlement to the dispute.[63]

Also, despite its revolutionary, direct action tactics, the IWW preached passive resistance in its disputes and gained the admiration of some religious and civil leaders who witnessed these long but peaceful strikes. During the Paterson, New Jersey, strike of 1913, Rabbi Leo Mannheimer praised the leadership of Bill Haywood, Elizabeth Gurley Flynn, and Carlo Tresca for keeping the 25,000 strikers peaceful, and the Paterson police chief reported absolutely no assaults on "scabs"—workers crossing picket lines, returning to work, and consequently breaking the strike.[64] On the whole, the Catholic Church had a negative view of the wobblies, and Catholic priests seldom supported their strikes because of the organization's avowed anarcho-syndicalism which promoted direct action, i.e., sabotage of the means of production.

The wobblies, however, soon declined in numbers as the public and employers reacted to the anarchists' refusal to support the efforts of the United States during World War I. Newspapers around the country criticized miners and lumbermen for sabotaging the war effort, but the IWW argued only for the fair treatment of working people. States enacted criminal syndicalism laws and the federal government produced the Sedition and Espionage Acts, using these acts to arrest numerous wobblies including Big Bill Haywood.[65] Samuel Gompers and the AFL disliked the wobblies immensely, but the wobblies clearly reminded him and other trade union leaders of the great mass of unorganized unskilled workers around the nation. Craft unions had failed to take up the banner of these workers who they considered to be unorganizable and obviously less skilled; in fact, the IWW likened the craft unionists to capitalists who feared the loss of their property.[66]

Throughout the conflict of World War I, the AFL supported the United States and acquiesced to the mediation services of the National War Labor Board. Of course the war gave labor additional leverage, and the government sought out the collaboration of organized labor to act as an intermediary with workers. The National War Labor Board, while promoting conciliation, acknowledged the right to organize, bargain collectively, and strike if necessary. How could working people agree to fight for liberty abroad if their own liberty to organize at home was denied? When the war ended, strikes broke out over wages that could not keep pace with inflation;

employers once again became antagonistic and because of Russian Bolshevism, a red scare began at home. Three hundred thousand steelworkers at U.S. Steel went out on strike for higher wages and an eight-hour day, but, using the forces of local, state, and national governments, the company broke the strike. If industrial unionization were to happen, it would depend on the successful organization of the steel industry.

Father Peter Dietz

During the first two decades of the twentieth century, the AFL had a great champion in Father Peter Dietz. His goal was to educate American workers in their right to organize and to maintain a Christian outlook in the union movement.[67] He wanted Catholic workers to maintain their Catholic identity in a country which had no faith-based unions, the form of worker associations preferred by Leo XIII. Dietz and sympathetic laypeople began organizing associations and disseminating literature on the social question. The German Catholic Central-Verein and the American Federation of Catholic Societies, organizations that Dietz helped lead, spoke out against economic injustices and educated their members in the abuses of capitalism and the dangers of socialism.[68]

Peter Dietz is most remembered for the Militia of Christ for Social Service, the Catholic labor group that operated in tandem with the wider labor movement, its purpose being the promotion of Catholic ethics within American labor. The Militia for Christ sponsored lectures at universities and colleges to encourage student participation in worker causes while discouraging affiliation with socialist endeavors. For clergy, it organized lectures, provided social-oriented sermons, and conducted retreats for trade unionists. The Militia for Christ also conducted social conferences for Catholic clergy and sponsored Labor Day Celebrations (*Social Service*, May 1911). The Catholic hierarchy welcomed the organization, and Catholic academics like Monsignor John Ryan embraced it,[69] although some in the labor movement and the Church requested a name change because they thought it was "too pious" sounding. The name was eventually changed to American Conference of Catholic Trade Unionists.[70] The socialist politician Victor Berger and intellectuals on the left were adamantly against cooperation between the labor movement and the Militia because of its sectarian nature.[71]

Dietz attended every AFL convention from 1909 to 1922, and he sometimes addressed the conventions, often fighting back attempts to dispel religious participation in the labor work.[72] Labor leaders in the American labor movement directed local and statewide bodies of the Militia of Christ. One of the leaders, John Mitchell of the United Mine Workers, commented:

> I believe that Catholic people should be in the vanguard in the movement for constructive social and industrial reform, and whether there be any justification for the charge there is a widespread impression that our Church is just a little over-conservative in matters of this kind; therefore, it seems to me that our people should adopt and pursue a systematic program for social betterment; that we should identify ourselves with the movement to promote legislation, that is, constructive legislation, for the protection of that great majority of the people in our country who are least able to protect themselves. The Militia of Christ for Social Service presents an avenue through which good work can be done for our less fortunate fellow beings, and at the same time credit can be reflected on the church itself.[73]

In 1915, Dietz also tried to create a formal relationship between the AFL and the American Federation of Catholic Societies to formulate joint positions on strikes, industrial education, social services, and other concerns. Samuel Gompers and his executive council, however, rejected any religious interference in the AFL.[74] Clearly, the labor movement valued the support of sympathetic Catholic clergy, but it did not want to lose its autonomy or cause sectarian divisions within its ranks.

Father Dietz agitated for a school of social science within the American Catholic Church to teach organizers, social workers, and others about Christian ethics and social-economic and political history. This idea would become the American Academy of Christian Democracy established in 1915. He later attempted to create a labor college within the structure of this academy, and some labor and Catholic Church leaders endorsed his vision. Nevertheless, the college closed its doors in 1922 after Bishop Moeller of Cincinnati forced Dietz to leave the diocese. Members of the Cincinnati Chamber of Commerce had complained to the bishop about Dietz's attacks on their support for the American Plan. Although never receiving the complete backing of the Catholic hierarchy, Dietz would see many of his ideas come to fruition in the National Catholic Welfare Conference: a bishops' pastoral letter on the social question, a national coordination committee for social issues, and the incorporation of laymen and women into the social justice work of the Church.

During this post–World War I period, the economic boom would end and unemployment would increase. The government also intervened to prevent strikes in coal mining and on the railways. Employers once again sought injunctive relief from the courts for the ostensible reason of protecting the citizens of the United States by preserving freedom of contract and defeating trusts (i.e., unions).

Notes

1. Melyvn Dubofsky and Foster Rhea Dulles, *Labor in America: A History*, 6th ed. (Wheeling, Ill.: Harlan Davidson, Inc., 1999), 8.

2. John R. Commons and Associates, *History of Labor in the United States*, as quoted in Henry Browne, *The Catholic Church and the Knights of Labor* (Washington, D.C.: The Catholic University of America Press, 1949), 7.

3. See *The Mystery of Capital* by Hernando de Soto for a description of the Homestead Act's importance in the development of American capitalism. The Homestead Act provided pioneers with land, making them property owners. They then invested themselves in the development of the land and created new wealth. Hernando de Soto makes a good case for the importance of property and the legal documentation of its ownership for economic development.

4. Dubofsky and Dulles, 81.

5. Henry J. Browne, *The Catholic Church and the Knights of Labor* (Washington, D.C.: The Catholic University of America Press, 1949), 6–7.

6. Joseph Quigley as quoted in Henry Browne, *The Catholic Church and the Knights of Labor* (Washington, D.C.: The Catholic University of America Press, 1949), 12–28.

7. Peter Guilday, *A History of the Councils of Baltimore, 1791–1884* (New York, 1933) as quoted in Henry Browne, *The Catholic Church and the Knights of Labor* (Washington, D.C.: The Catholic University of America Press, 1949), 10.

8. Patrick Healy, "Catholic Economic Thought," *Catholic Builders of the Nation*, 111, Boston, 1923, 10, as quoted in Henry Browne, *The Catholic Church and the Knights of Labor* (Washington, D.C.: The Catholic University of America Press, 1949), 12.

9. Henry J. Browne, *The Catholic Church and the Knights of Labor* (Washington, D.C.: The Catholic University of America Press, 1949), 13–15.

10. Ibid., 16–17.

11. Terence Powderly, *Thirty Years of Labor 1859–1889*, Philadelphia, Pa.: By the Author, 1890: reprint (New York: Augustus M. Kelley Publishers), 31–32.

12. Dubofsky and Dulles, 91.

13. Ibid., 92.

14. Ibid., 113.

15. Fergus MacDonald, C.P., *The Catholic Church and the Secret Societies in the United States*, New York, 1946, 51, as quoted in Henry Browne, *The Catholic Church and the Knights of Labor* (Washington, D.C.: The Catholic University of America Press, 1949), 21.

16. Browne, 24–25.

17. Powderly, 44.

18. Dubofsky and Dulles, 119.

19. Kim Voss, *The Making of Exceptionalism: The Knights of Labor and Class Formation in the Nineteenth Century* (Ithaca, N.Y.: Cornell University Press, 1993), 82.

20. Ibid., 28.

21. Browne, 40–60.

22. Craig Phelan, *GrandMaster Workman: Terence Powderly and the Knights of Labor* (Westport, Conn.: Greenwood Press, 2000), 112–13.

23. Ibid., 188–90.

24. *Freeman's Journal*, April 3, 1886, from *New York Sun* dispatch of St. Louis, March 26, 1886.

25. Browne, 96.

26. Ibid., 108.

27. Ibid., 164.

28. Ibid., 166.

29. Ibid., 219.

30. Ibid., 244–46.

31. Robert Weir, *Beyond Labor's Veil: The Culture of the Knights of Labor* (University Park: Pennsylvania State University Press, 1996), 20.

32. Powderly, 307.

33. Ibid., 310.

34. Weir, 37.

35. Ibid., 100.

36. Voss, 173.

37. Ibid., 171.

38. Dubofsky and Dulles, 130.

39. Ibid., 137.

40. Powderly, 234.

41. Dubofsky and Dulles, 146.

42. Phelan, 138–41.

43. Voss, 202.

44. Ibid., 204.

45. Ibid.

46. John Laslett, "Samuel Gompers and the Rise of American Business Unionism," in *Labor Leaders in America*, ed. Melvyn Dubofsky and Warren Van Tine, 62–68 (Urbana: University of Illinois, 1987), 75.

47. Dubofsky and Dulles, 153.

48. Ibid., 161.

49. Laslett, 63.

50. Ibid., 66.

51. Powderly letter to Tom O'Reilly, as quoted in Phelan, 2000, 248.

52. Laslett, 70.

53. Roger Finke and Rodney Stark, *The Churching of America, 1776–1990: Winners and Losers in Our Religious Economy* (New Brunswick, N.J.: Rutgers University Press, 1992), 115–19.

54. Dubofsky and Dulles, 188.

55. Laslett, 76.

56. Dubofsky and Dulles, 180.

57. Ibid.

58. Ibid., 187.

59. Ibid., 189.

60. Mort Gerberg, *The U.S. Constitution for Everyone* (New York: The Berkeley Publishing Co., 1987,) 49.

61. Melvyn Dubofsky, *We Shall Be All: A History of the Industrial Workers of the World*, 2nd ed. (Urbana: University of Illinois Press, 1988), 22.

62. Lewis E. Palmer, "A Strike for Four Loaves of Bread," *Survey*, XXVVII, Feb. 3, 1912 as quoted in *We Shall Be All: A History of the Industrial Workers of the World*, 245. 2nd ed. (Urbana: University of Illinois Press, 1988).

63. Paul Stroh C.SS.R., *The Catholic Clergy and American Labor Disputes: 1900–1913*. Unpublished Ph.D. dissertation, Department of Economics. The Catholic University of America, 1939, as quoted in Mary Harrita Fox, *Peter E. Dietz, Labor Priest,* 41 (Notre Dame, Ind.: University of Notre Dame Press, 1953).

64. Leo Mannheimer, "Darkest New Jersey," *Independent*, LXXIV, 1190–1191, as quoted in *We Shall Be All: A History of the Industrial Workers of the World*, 2nd ed. (Urbana: University of Illinois Press, 1988), 245.

65. Dubofsky and Dulles, 207.

66. Ibid., 199.

67. Mary Harrita Fox, *Peter E. Dietz, Labor Priest* (Notre Dame, Ind.: University of Notre Dame, 1953), 14.

68. Ibid., 33.

69. Ibid., 48–49.

70. Ibid., 64.

71. Ibid., 52.

72. Ibid., 44.

73. Mitchell to Dietz, June 1, 1911, quoted in Mary Harrita Fox, *Peter E. Dietz Labor Priest*, 52.

74. Mary Harrita Fox, 118–20.

~

CHAPTER FOUR

World War I Social Reconstruction

The Influence of Monsignor John Ryan on the Social Question

Monsignor John Ryan is the stellar figure in the development of Catholic social thought in the United States, which addresses directly the needs of workers and their families. He grew up as a Minnesota farm boy in a devout Catholic family that produced another priest and two Roman Catholic nuns. As a child he listened to the local farmers criticize railroad monopolies, and his father William was a member of the National Farmers Alliance, a group that decried these monopolies as well. Ryan also read the *Irish World and Industrial Liberator* which supported the Knights of Labor and other groups that organized against the industrial titans.[1] As he moved through his priestly formation in the 1890s, he came to identify with the more liberal wing of the Catholic Church that encouraged greater involvement of the Church in U.S. culture and social reforms. Pope Leo XIII promulgated the papal encyclical *Rerum Novarum* during Ryan's seminary training which was contemporaneous with the growth of populism in the nation.[2] *Rerum Novarum* maintained the right of private property and repudiated the socialist vision of social ownership, but it also harshly criticized the owners of production for their treatment of workers and advocated state intervention in the economy for the good of the community. Ryan had found a Catholic document that made his populist and then progressive leanings acceptable to his Catholic faith. He would become a bridge between American progressivism and the American Catholic Church.

American progressives, primarily Protestant faithful like social gospelers and muckrakers, had many differences to bridge with urban Roman Catholics. The progressive activists, clergy, and thinkers tended to be middle class and native-born. The Catholics were working class and foreign-born. The progressives championed a vision of a social commonwealth based on economic democracy, not union organizing. The working class Roman Catholics needed better wages and working conditions immediately and filled the union halls. Progressives with nativist views saw the Catholic Church as partly to blame for the poverty of its members because the Church rejected modernity. Furthermore, some nativists argued that one could not be both Catholic and American because a Catholic's allegiance was to the Roman Pontiff. On the Catholic side, the leadership suspected that the Protestant social gospelers who entered the industrial slums only sought converts. The unfortunate upshot for the Catholic Church was that a fear of losing its flock to Protestant churches and socialists made it appear anti-reformist.[3] John Ryan would find himself working to bridge the gulf between these two groups.

Rerum Novarum gave Ryan the Church teaching that he needed to make his connection. The encyclical continued in the Thomistic theological tradition, and it argued for the state to have a role in reform.[4] Ryan had already come to the conclusion that the social question was a moral one and not simply an economic one by reading the works of progressive economist Richard Ely and the moral thinking of William Lilly, an English Catholic who looked at all social institutions through the lens of moral values. Progressivism offered some means of unity with Catholic social thought because it offered a revisionist understanding of natural law that meshed with the theology of St. Thomas Aquinas. The laissez-faire extremism found in the United States had developed from a view of natural law that was too dependent on the Enlightenment philosophy of John Locke. Capitalists had promoted individual liberties (and abuses) by stressing self-interest and negative, non-interventionist government to their extremes. The progressives returned to the writings of the founding fathers and discovered political thought that balanced natural rights and social responsibility. Ryan's anti-Lockean Catholicism also struck this balance.[5] Without a doubt, American progressivism had conditioned Ryan's thought, and Ryan was comfortable reading behind the text of Aquinas's *Summa Theologica* to make his point. His contribution is immense to the American Catholic Church's engagement in the social question. He took three main points from *Rerum Novarum*: (1) The social question is not merely economic, it is also a moral question; (2) traditional Catholic moral tradition is brought to bear on the modern world through scholastic principles; and (3) state intervention is sometimes necessary for social amelioration.[6]

> In his fundamental thought, then, Ryan discovered and articulated the keystone of his ethical system: The nature of man was sacred because it was created by God and destined for life—reasonable life. From this fundamental truth followed the ethical principle that the universally equal dignity of the human person (his person and his rights) had to be preserved and fostered. Any actions that violated that dignity or abridged the rights supporting or ensuring its maintenance were to be condemned in the strongest possible way. At the most basic level, then, Ryan discovered a significant point of contact between the Catholic and American reform systems of thought: both were insistent that the dignity of the individual was inviolable.[7]

Ryan's contribution to the social question was based on faith and reason. God created human beings to live reasonable lives. To live a reasonable life required a state because human beings are social beings, and by their nature they seek out some authority. The authority of the state comes from God, but it only has this authority so as to promote the well-being of its members—i.e., help them lead a reasonable life. Ryan argues that without a state human beings cannot achieve what is necessary to live this life.[8]

Ryan published his dissertation, A Living Wage: Its Ethical and Economic Aspects, in 1906. He argued that a living wage was one of the requirements for a reasonable life in an industrial society. The state had the responsibility to see that employees received living wages. In an industrial society, a living wage was primary because the human right to life could only be understood in economic terms.[9] Natural law thinking, therefore, had social utility, but Ryan had added the notion of "expediency" to the natural law ideas of harmony and balance. American Catholicism needed to address the social question, and Rerum Novarum's use of Thomism and its acceptance of state intervention provided the aperture. Ryan promoted state participation in industrial affairs while having a healthy Catholic fear of an all-encompassing state. With Ryan's thinking, Catholics began to make greater connections with the social initiatives of American progressives.[10]

John Ryan later became a spokesperson for minimum wage fights in states across the country, and he authored a 1911 initiative in his home state of Minnesota. The legislature passed a revised version in 1913.[11] He was a friend of labor unions but not a labor union activist. The unions had not achieved a living wage or a reasonable life for workers through strikes or collective bargaining. Although aware of the impediments to successful labor organizing, he focused his efforts on legislative reforms.[12] His voluminous writings included common points with some American progressives: "public ownership of public utilities; public ownership of mines and forests; control of monopolies, either by breaking them or fixing their prices; progressive income and inheritance taxes; taxation of the future increase in land values; prohibition of speculation on the stock and commodity exchanges."[13]

Monsignor Ryan was important to the post–World War I era because he authored the American Bishop's Program on Social Reconstruction of 1919. The American Catholic Church had become more acceptable to non-Catholics because it had actively supported the war effort. As during most war periods, the state and big business had granted social reforms (e.g., the National War Labor Board, which mediated industrial disputes) to keep the military/industrial machine running. The Catholic Church and labor approved of Woodrow Wilson's progressivism in this regard. Once the war had ended, however, the business community and state once again took a hard line against labor; for example, business groups like the U.S. Chamber of Commerce endorsed the American Plan which hoped to keep industry free of unions by maintaining the open shop.

Nevertheless, toward the end of the war and after, Church leaders, government officials, and other liberal thinkers had begun to consider the postwar reconstruction period both in Europe and the United States as an ideal moment for social reform. Protestant evangelist Sherwood Eddy and other progressive thinkers believed the forces mustered during the war could be channeled into a crusade to reconstruct a more just society at home.[14] Progressives hoped that political democracy would lead to industrial democracy. Some social gospelers who had eschewed an alliance with labor because of labor's selfish nature now attempted a working relationship. The Federal Council of Churches actively supported the ideal of industrial democracy, including the living wage and collective bargaining (Committee on the War and the Religious Outlook, *Church and Industrial Reconstruction* 1920, 11–12, 108). Of course, conservative churches and business people criticized these progressive ideas as socialistic.[15]

The Catholic Church was now a more mainstream institution, and the hierarchy desired a reconstruction position of its own. The bishops wanted to check radicalism and secure the working class for the Church; in addition, a letter would promote the Catholic Church as a valued member of American society.[16] The Reverend John O'Grady, the head of the Bishops' Committee on Special War Activities, asked John Ryan to write the document for the bishops. Ryan had written a rough paper already, and Reverend O'Grady literally saw it sitting on Ryan's desk. With a few changes and additions, it became the first pastoral letter of the American bishops.

The letter borrowed much from American progressivism, but Ryan found support for his positions in the Leonine tradition (i.e., Leo XIII's views on the social question in particular). Ryan wanted to make the National War Labor Board a permanent agency as well as maintain the National Employment Service. Moreover, he wanted the reforms to lead to greater cooperation between management and labor because industrial peace could only come when workers became at least co-owners of the means of production.[17] He borrowed the ideas on cooperatives from a group of twenty British Quaker industrialists who advocated worker-ownership and promoted an altruistic spirit based on modest living.[18] The Bishops' Committee advocated a number of reforms: land colonization; retention of the National Employment Service; retirement of women workers from industrial work; retention of the National War Labor Board; a living wage; government housing for workers; government check of monopolies; development of cooperative stores (modeled after Britain's Rochdale stores); social insurance against injury, illness, unemployment, and old age; labor participation in management; vocational training for children; and child labor laws.[19]

The reaction to the program was praise from progressives and radicals. Upton Sinclair called it the "Catholic miracle."[20] Conservatives inside and outside of the Church decried what they saw as Marxism, and Catholic Church conservatives called it a violation of canon law.[21] Ryan and the bishops who signed the letter referred to *Rerum Novarum* and natural law theory and underscored the moral rather than the canonical importance of the letter. Nevertheless, reformers would not see any reconstruction because the economic power of business interests would devour their attempts at moral and rational suasion.

During the 1920s, labor also faced the onslaught of Taylorism and welfare capitalism—corporate forms of progressivism. While Taylorism attempted to make work more efficient and productive, welfare capitalism offered employees insurance, health care, recreational opportunities, and other benefits to make them feel more like members of an organization rather than a commodity. Unfortunately, a company could just as soon take benefits away as provide them. Company unions encouraged worker participation and greater identity with the employer and, of course, during the relatively good economic days of the early 1920s, workers responded to these rights given as gifts. Union membership decreased at the beginning of the 1920s.

Unions had roughly 5,000,000 members at the beginning of the decade, but by 1929 the number had fallen to 3,443,000. Anti-union groups like the National Association of Manufacturers, a very conservative association of business people, had promoted the open shop through the American

Plan, and periodicals continued to disparage the labor movement as being communistic or corrupt. Although there were communist sympathizers who were unionists and some unions were strong-armed by gangsters, the press exaggerated their influence. By discrediting unionists, the owners of capital defeated attempts at establishing democracy at the workplace through collective bargaining. The workers did not garner the passion necessary to promote stronger unions or to fight for political gains for labor. Pro-labor Senator Robert La Follette from Wisconsin, despite support from the American Federation of Labor (AFL), did not have a significant impact on the 1924 presidential election, and conservative pundits mocked the progressive dud.[22] There would be no true social reconstruction in the 1920s, and progressives, including John Ryan and progressive Catholic bishops, had lost a window of opportunity.

The onslaught of the Great Depression would not raise up a mighty front of the laboring class despite the fifteen million unemployed and a drop of $40 billion in national income.[23] In spite of the propaganda and flurry of communist organizing, extreme radicals who hoped for a revolution found their call falling on the deaf ears of working people. Communists were "day dreaming."[24] With a deteriorating economy, employees avoided strikes while watching their welfare capitalism benefits and jobs being cut. William Green, Gomper's successor as president of the AFL, was promoting a shorter workweek, but he refused to back calls for an unemployment insurance program being touted by some politicians and progressives, including Monsignor John Ryan and the American Catholic bishops. Green followed Gomper's conservative view of the government's involvement in employment questions. Some states passed worker compensation laws, and Wisconsin passed an unemployment insurance law. In 1932, Congress passed the Norris-La Guardia Act which prohibited yellow-dog contracts, prohibited the use of injunctions against labor groups except in specific situations, and most importantly acknowledged the right of workers to associate.

Putting people back to work for Franklin D. Roosevelt meant he had to give greater freedom to industry to develop its own codes of business while giving employees the explicit right to organize and bargain collectively. He achieved these ends in the National Industrial Recovery Act (NIRA) which the Supreme Court found unconstitutional. The NIRA also failed because employers, when developing their industry's codes, manipulated the codes to prevent individual employees from exercising their supposed right to concerted activity. For instance, merit became the basis for all wages, benefits, and job promotions, and, of course, the employers could always find union sympathizers to have no merit.[25]

John Ryan, now in his sixties, and the staffs of the National Catholic Welfare Conference and its Social Action Department, heartily endorsed most of FDR's policies. Ryan opposed the Economy Act that cut the salaries of government employees but approved of the National Industrial Recovery Bill to jump-start the economy. Ryan, however, saw a thirty-hour workweek and a minimum wage law as the best means to help the economy.[26] In the first few months of the New Deal, the National Recovery Administration's public relations office asked him to write a letter encouraging clergy to support its work. Secretary of Labor Francis Perkins appointed him to the advisory council of the U.S. Employment Service.[27]

John Ryan became a diplomat for the New Deal with the Catholic community. In *Commonweal* in April 1934, he argued that the New Deal effectuated the proper role of the state in serving the economic needs of the country. The legislation did not sanction rampant individualism nor did it fall into the inefficiencies of state-controlled socialism. Labor had a role in the direction and governance of industries. He called the New Deal a via media between capitalism and communism.[28] Ryan had seen progressive ideas stymied after World War I, and he wanted to do everything possible to make them a reality now. In 1934, General Hugh S. Johnson appointed Ryan a member of the Industrial Appeals Board of the National Industrial Recovery Act, and he remained so until the Supreme Court found the NIRA unconstitutional in 1935. In a press release after the unconstitutionality decision, Ryan called for increased union membership and general wage and hour contracts to improve the difficult situation of workers (National Catholic Welfare Conference press release May 29, 1935). The New Deal was the result of the efforts of middle class reformers like John Ryan and Protestant progressives and not the labor movement.

A Change in Law Aids the Organizing Drives of the 1930s

It was the Wagner Act, sponsored by Senator Robert Wagner of New York, that brought equality to organized labor. Although at first not supported by Roosevelt, he would later embrace the act because it offered a balanced weight to the power of employers. Earlier in the New Deal, the NIRA trade associations could not institute industrial codes benefiting business without granting to employees the right to bargain collectively. The Wagner Act, however, was truly pro-labor legislation. Up until its passage, despite good intentions, no previous legislation had actually given employees the right to engage in concerted activity and at the same time made it illegal for employers to refuse to negotiate with union representatives. The Wagner Act outlawed company unions without giving any concessions to employers and prohibited the coercion of employees in the exercise of their right to associate. The National Labor Relations Board (NLRB) conducted representation elections, heard unfair labor practice charges, sought remedies, and had the power to ask for federal injunctions when management committed unfair labor practices.[29] Yet companies continued to combat unions with anti-union propaganda, labor spies, bribery, and other questionable means. They refused to bargain with their employees' representatives believing the Wagner Act would be found unconstitutional, but it was found constitutional in *N.L.R.B. v. Jones and Laughlin Steel Company* in 1937.[30]

Public opinion polls favored the Roosevelt administration's furthering of labor's power. The administration believed that industrial stability would result when labor and management were put on equal footing. And despite numerous work stoppages, the public's opinion remained with labor and the birth of the Congress of Industrial Organizations (CIO). *Social Justice*, a periodical of Father Charles Coughlin's Detroit-based National Union for Social Justice, complained that communists led the CIO. John Ryan, however, felt this was red-baiting by those who wished to defeat any efforts for social justice, and he compared this red scare rhetoric to efforts to defeat the Knights of Labor in the 1880s. The Catholic bishops refused to condemn the CIO, and Archbishop Edward Mooney of Detroit stated that the influence of communists in the CIO was too small to be taken seriously.[31] At this point, Ryan and Catholic progressives had a firm hold on the direction of the American Church in the area of industrial relations. During this time, Father John Hayes of the Social Action Department of the U.S. Conference of Catholic Bishops distributed *Social Action Notes for Priests* to keep clergy informed of the work of other religious and laypeople in the labor movement.[32]

John L. Lewis led the CIO with power in mind while William Green, president of the AFL, preached consensus and cooperation. Lewis led as an opportunist, realizing that power tactics and conflict played roles in organizing the mass production industries. The CIO's success proved Green wrong because his leadership by moral suasion was seen as empty.[33] It was a middle class, non-working class position that failed to address the immediate demands of the workers.

Organizing along industrial lines, the CIO had 3,700,000 members to the AFL's 3,400,000 by 1937.[34] The International Ladies' Garment Workers later returned to the AFL, but the other industrial unions became the Congress of Industrial Organizations. Philip Murray, Lewis' lieutenant in the United Mine Workers (UMW), had begun organizing in the steel industry in 1936. Within a few months, the major steel companies had recognized the CIO and the Steel Workers Organizing Committee as the collective bargaining agent of the steel workers. The U.S. Steel Corporation quickly agreed to 10 percent wage increases and the forty-hour week.[35] The Steel Workers Organizing Committee found it much harder to organize the Little Steel companies who used anti-union tactics and unsympathetic citizen associations to stymie the organizing. Yet by 1941, the NLRB had forced the Little Steel companies to recognize the United Steelworkers of America as well.[36]

Similarly, the United Automobile Workers of America (UAW) used the sit-down strike to gain recognition of their union. In 1937, John L. Lewis and General Motors (GM) president William Knudsen met with the Michigan governor to avert any violence at the Flint, Michigan, sit-down strike that ultimately ended after forty-four days. Chrysler soon followed GM in recognizing the union, and Ford would be organized after four more years. Unions and workers relinquished the sit-down tactic once the courts fully approved the NLRB since the Board could then conduct its representation elections without interference.[37] Of course, the rivalry between the AFL and the CIO led to jurisdictional disputes some of which according to Dubofsky and Dulles were more acrimonious than the conflicts between labor and capital.[38]

In 1936, the CIO also established the Non-Partisan League to promote labor's needs in the political arena. The New Deal had been good for labor, and the CIO wanted to insure the support of friendly politicians in the future. William Green was adamantly against such political work although some of the AFL-affiliated unions supported the efforts. Franklin D. Roosevelt won the 1936 election, and students of politics attribute his win to the efforts of organized labor.[39] Some thought that this success could lead to the development of a labor party, but the AFL remained opposed to such intentions; it was simply easier to support friends of labor and oppose labor's enemies. The history of the U.S. labor movement had already shown that the workers themselves were not interested in focusing on class divisions or the championing of a socialist society.[40] Although socialists and communists played significant roles in union organizing, they did not capture the hearts and minds of the working class. Many Irish Catholics participated in the UAW organizing drives, and they later formed the Association of Catholic Trade Unionists (ACTU), a group that denounced socialism and communism but strongly supported the UAW.[41]

On the one hand, John L. Lewis, without supporting their ideologies, used many labor radicals and communists for their organizing skills, while also being aware of their desire to influence the CIO and the Non-Partisan League. On the other hand, Philip Murray, president of the CIO in its most tumultuous decade, and Sidney Hillman, the first vice president of the

CIO, worked against any attempts at communist influence. Murray's work against communism was in part due to his anti-Marxist Roman Catholic advisors.[42] Also, the work of the Catholic labor schools (organized to educate unionists), the Catholic Worker movement, and other progressive, non-socialist religious efforts impeded the boring-from-within strategy of the far left. Lewis had begun to believe he might have a political career as a running mate with President Roosevelt, but the president never pursued this possibility. By 1940, John L. Lewis no longer supported Roosevelt and vowed he would resign as president of the CIO if Roosevelt were to win reelection, which he did.[43] Lewis had lost the opportunity to move labor forward in the political front and had lost the opportunity to reunite the AFL and the CIO on the labor front.

During the organizing drives of the 1930s and the 1940s, the CIO had the support of the Catholic Worker movement and Catholic labor schools. Lay Catholic Dorothy Day and Peter Maurin, the founders of the Catholic Worker movement, had a distinct view about the social direction of the Catholic community. Their perspective had an ethical purity that limited the movement's impact on organized labor. As Christian idealists, they saw unionism as a stopgap measure to alleviate industrial injustices, and they promoted an organic medieval-like guild system of worklife and agrarian cooperatives, which some critics saw as romantic folly. Peter Maurin at times spoke out against strikes, and Dorothy Day, although an early supporter of the CIO organizing, found the power of organized labor to be foreign to the gospel message. The endorsement of cooperatives, small shopkeepers, and artisan guilds resonates with the commonwealth vision of Terence Powderly and the Knights of Labor. In effect, the Catholic Workers envisioned an industrial commonwealth where the worker would lie down with the capitalist. The Catholic Worker organized hospitality houses around the country which became centers of "radical" Christian thought in American Catholicism: ex-seminarians, Catholic unionists, and the unemployed discussed the social dilemmas of the era at these hospitality houses. The Workers were radical because they believed in a new social economic system, lived austere lives in common, and dedicated themselves to serving the poor. They were orthodox because they faithfully prayed together, received the sacraments, and respected both the tradition and hierarchy of the Catholic Church.

The philosophy of personalism, as developed by Catholic French philosopher Emmanuel Mounier, had reached its peak of popularity during the 1920s and 1930s but continued to influence the Catholic left throughout the 1940s and 1950s. Personalism focused on the primacy of the person as a free spiritual being. The human being seeks integration in all aspects of his or her life to reach a state of harmony with creation. Personalism did not box human beings into any particular political, social, or historical moment.[44] For personalists, and therefore many Catholic Workers, work should be a vocation of artisanship and not mechanistic slavery. Furthermore, in the thralls of the Great Depression, millions of God's sons and daughters lacked work. Up until this time, American Catholicism unlike European Catholicism had not taken ownership of the Church's social teachings but Americans never had to respond to powerful communist parties and communist led unions.

The Catholic Worker movement gave some social justice oriented Catholics the means to confront the evils they encountered during those harsh economic days. The Catholic Worker newspaper taught the social encyclicals to many American Catholics, and the community modeled Christian charity. In addition, Neo-Thomist philosopher Jacques Maritain and other Catholic intellectuals visited Catholic Worker houses sharing their insights and animating the communities to embrace living out the gospel message.

This radical lay Catholic movement distanced itself from labor at the end of the 1930s because Catholic Workers believed the AFL and the CIO had acquiesced to the capitalist system by treating labor as a commodity rather than as a gift from God.[45] Although the Catholic Workers' influence in the labor arena dwindled with time, resurfacing during the United Farm Workers struggles of the 1960s and 1970s, former Catholic Workers did establish new organizations and periodicals to support labor unions.

John Cort, a Harvard educated Catholic Worker, co-founded the Association of Catholic Trade Unionists (ACTU) in 1937. The ACTU had affiliates throughout the East and Midwest, and the Association required membership in a union. The group not only sponsored labor schools that taught organizing methods, bargaining skills, and speech making, but it also actively supported striking workers. "Like their parent Catholic Workers, the ACTists were especially effective in swinging Catholic moral prestige behind particular strikes, with the added advantage that ACTU operated from within labor's ranks."[46] During the 1940s, the ACTU concentrated on impeding the work of communist organizers within unions and sympathized with the union movement's desire for more military production. Dorothy Day rejected both of these positions because communist organizers had energy and commitment to offer and Catholic workers in her opinion could only be pacifists; the gulf between the Catholic Worker movement and the ACTU widened. John Cort's *Labor Leader* also accepted industrialization so long as employers paid a "living wage," and he looked to a time when managers and employees would have industry councils to plan together the production and sale of their goods and services.[47] The industry councils, coming from Catholic corporatist thinking, would have brought together responsible union and management representatives to seek out agreeable and effective solutions to mutual concerns.[48] John Cort and the ACTists cited the social encyclicals, particularly *Quadragesimo Anno* (1931), to support the Catholic character of their views on the labor movement.

Although the ACTU is sometimes painted as a conservative tool of anticommunist Catholicism, it was not directed by the hierarchy or clerical reactionaries. The ACTU sided with Catholic gravediggers in their strike against the archdiocese of New York in 1949, and both the ACTU and Archbishop Edward Mooney spoke out against the anti-labor fulminations of Father Charles Coughlin.[49]

The struggle between Catholic American liberalism, one that included John Ryan and John Cort, and Catholic idealism exemplified by Dorothy Day and Peter Maurin, points to the challenge of recognizing both the material benefits of technology and industrialism while acknowledging their sometimes spiritual emptiness (i.e., the alienation of the worker). Dorothy Day wrote: "Labor is a discipline imposed on all of us because of the Fall, but it is also a vocation . . . whereby man shares in God's creative activity. . . . It is not the low pay and rough conditions of modern factory work but the lack of responsibility that is devastating. The worker feels little relationship to the human and social consequences of what he produces."[50]

The Catholic Worker also spawned the liberal Catholic Labor Association of Chicago that recognized the fundamentally conservative nature of American workers who wanted to share the rewards of capitalism and not destroy it. Similarly, Fathers Charles Owen Rice and Carl Hensler, the famous Pittsburgh labor priests, became more estranged from the Catholic Worker as they participated in the day-to-day efforts of organizing steel workers with the CIO. They, too, recognized the basic conservatism of the workers they met.[51] Furthermore, as American Catholicism and the labor movement passed into the 1950s, the urgency of organizing workers declined because collective bargaining became relatively accepted by both management and labor and prosperity dampened labor's activism. If labor could consistently win wage and benefit gains and management could afford automatic increases, the religious radicals and liberals saw no urgency in championing the rights of American workers. Both liberal and radical Catholic groups turned more of their attention to civil rights and peace movements. Radical Catholics, moreover, could not accept unions that sometimes operated discriminatory hiring halls or gained power and wealth through military production.

Notes

1. Francis L. Broderick, *Right Reverend New Dealer John Ryan* (New York: Macmillan Co., 1963), 8.

2. Ibid., 14–18.

3. Joseph McShane, *"Sufficiently Radical" Catholicism, Progressivism, and the Bishops' Pastoral Program of 1919* (Washington, D.C.: The Catholic University of America Press, 1986), 14–15.

4. Ibid., 29.

5. Ibid., 33.

6. Ibid., 31.

7. Ibid., 40.

8. Ibid., 40.

9. Ibid., 43.

10. Ibid., 42–43.

11. Broderick, 82.

12. Broderick, 58.

13. Broderick, 59.

14. McShane, 97.

15. Ibid., 124.

16. Ibid., 147.

17. Ibid., 151.

18. McShane, 159.

19. Ibid., 161–66.

20. McShane, 197.

21. McShane, 212.

22. Dubofsky and Dulles, 241.

23. Ibid., 244.

24. Louis Adamic, *My America: 1928–1938* (New York: Harper & Brothers Publishers, 1938), 333–37.

25. Dubofsky and Dulles, 254.

26. Broderick, 212–13.

27. Ibid., 214.

28. John Ryan, "The New Deal and Social Justice," *Commonweal*, April 13, 1934, 657–59, as quoted in Francis Broderick, *Right Reverend New Dealer John Ryan* (New York: Macmillan Co., 1963), 216.

29. Dubofsky and Dulles, 260.

30. Ibid., 264.

31. Broderick, 234–35.

32. George Higgins with William Bole, *Organized Labor in the Church* (New York: Paulist Press, 1993), 54.

33. Craig Phelan, "William Green and the Ideal of Christian Cooperation," in *Labor Leaders in America*, ed. Melvyn Dubofsky and Warren Van Tine (Urbana: University of Illinois, 1987), 156.

34. Dubofsky and Dulles, 282.

35. Ibid., 288.

36. Foster Rhea Dulles, *Labor in America: A History*, 3rd. ed. (New York: Thomas Y. Crowell Co., 1966), 302.

37. Dubofsky and Dulles, 290.

38. Ibid., 291.

39. Ibid., 296.

40. Ibid., 298.

41. Nelson Lichtenstein, *The Most Dangerous Man in Detroit: Walter Reuther and the Fate of American Labor* (New York: HarperCollins Publishers, 1995), 187–89.

42. Dubofsky and Dulles, 299.

43. Dubofsky and Dulles, 303.

44. Mel Piehl, *Breaking Bread: The Catholic Worker and the Origin of Catholic Radicalism* (Philadelphia, Penn.: Temple University Press, 1982), 70.

45. Piehl, 125.

46. Ibid., 70.

47. Piehl, 164.

48. Dorothy Day, "On Distributism: Answer to John Cort," *The Catholic Worker*, Dec. 1948, 1, 3, http://www.catholicworker.org/dorothyday/ (visited on Jun. 8, 2005).

49. Higgins, 61.

50. Dorothy Day, *Catholic Worker*, 12 (Nov. 1945), 3; 14 (Mar. 1948), 1; 5 (Dec. 1937), 1; as quoted in Mel Piehl, *Breaking Bread: The Catholic Worker and the Origin of Catholic Radicalism* (Philadelphia, Penn.: Temple University Press, 1982), 163.

51. Piehl, 167–68.

CHAPTER FIVE

~

U.S. Labor 1940s to 2000

Catholic Labor Schools, Business Unionism, the UFW, and the Plant Closures Decade

Labor's Apogee

At the 1940 Congress of Industrial Organizations (CIO) convention Philip Murray, successor to John L. Lewis as president of the CIO, would lead the CIO's prevailing anti-communist position by calling for a convention wide vote disassociating the organization from communism and all other foreign ideologies. Murray supported the defense efforts of the federal administration. In 1941, Lewis again dominated national news when the United Mine Workers (UMW) demanded the union shop in the coal mines controlled by Big Steel. This demand was made before the National Defense Mediation Board which had been created to prevent labor stoppages in vital industries while war loomed on the horizon. When the board denied the union shop, the UMW made a strike call, and Lewis browbeat President Roosevelt into setting up a tribunal that was in essence pro-labor. The three-person tribunal gave the UMW its union shop but also cost the labor movement support in Washington and around the country. The House soon passed a bill that outlawed all strikes over the union shop or union jurisdiction in the defense industries. Moreover, strike votes in these industries had to come after a thirty-day cooling-off period and with government supervised elections.[1] With the onset of World War II, labor, government, and management formed a three-point plan for industrial peace: (1) no strikes; (2) create a tripartite board of labor, management, and public; and (3) peaceful settlement of disputes. As a whole, organized labor did support the war effort, and the key to the agreement was the National War Labor Board whose primary job was to take over all unsettled industrial disputes.

Post–World War II America saw a resurgence of labor demands and 2,000,000 industrial workers on strike by the close of 1945. President Truman tried to prevent industrial strife by calling a labor-management conference that ended without success. He also used injunctions against the UMW and took over the railroads when negotiations between railroad workers and the railways broke down. The strikes during the post-war period solidified labor's power and its role in the American economy. The war production demands provided labor an opportunity for expansion. Some clergy became noted arbitrators and mediators like Monsignor Francis Haas of the Catholic University of America's School of Social Science. He helped settle hundreds of labor disputes from the mid-1930s into the 1950s. In 1943, he became director of the federal government's Fair Employment Practices Commission, but within a few months stepped down from the position when named bishop of Grand Rapids, Michigan.[2]

Later Congress enacted the anti-labor Taft-Hartley Act in 1947 by overriding President Truman's veto. The Act made it an unfair labor practice for unions to coerce employees to become union members, required a sixty-day notification before striking (a cooling-off period), protected management rights in collective bargaining, and made it illegal for unions to refuse to bargain. The greatest blow to the union movement was outlawing the closed shop, making the union shop harder to obtain through complicated election procedures, and giving the states the ability to ban the union shop (i.e., right-to-work legislation).[3] The Taft-Hartley Act also contained provisions for presidential interventions in labor disputes causing a national emergency, the establishment of the Federal Mediation and Conciliation Service, and a General Counsel to enforce the labor law.

Catholic Labor Schools

Jesuits in the United States had become the largest of the Society of Jesus' national bodies by the 1930s, making up one-fifth of the Jesuit order worldwide.[4] The heady days of the New Deal and the CIO campaigns to organize industrial workers pulled Jesuits as well as other Catholic religious into the service of the laboring class, a class from which many of them had come. Jesuits first organized labor schools in New York, and the effort spread to other Eastern and Midwestern cities. Fathers Joe Coogan and John Coffield, both Los Angeles diocesan priests, continued this trend with their labor school work on Brooklyn Avenue in East Los Angeles between

1941 and 1943. Father Coogan, who had studied at the Catholic University of America in Washington, brought the night school, adult education format to Los Angeles. In addition, Father Bill McIntosh, SJ, a professor at Loyola University, eventually metamorphosed his labor school work into a professional school of industrial relations; later, he worked in the field of human/race relations. Policeman Tom Bradley, the future mayor of Los Angeles, was among his students.[5]

Jesuit labor priests attempted to give life to the Church's social teaching by providing classes on the social encyclicals, particularly *Rerum Novarum* and *Quadragesimo Anno*, and hiring qualified Catholic laypeople to teach the intricacies of contract negotiations, grievance procedures, and parliamentary rules of order. Leo XIII in *Rerum Novarum* permitted Catholic workers to join worker associations to counterbalance the immense economic power of employers in the late nineteenth century. Pope Pius XI wrote *Quadragesimo Anno* forty years later in 1931 to show continued support for unions and suggest alternative guild-like economic institutions to secure the well-being of both employers and employees. The Fordham School of Workers in New York, organized by Jesuits, rented space to Catholic lay activist Dorothy Day and the Catholic Worker movement; the two groups soon went in their own directions. The labor school Jesuits structured their curriculum with the nuts and bolts of contract negotiations, labor politics, and anti-communism because the utopian corporatism promoted by *Quadragesimo Anno* seemed unrealistic in the American context. The Catholic Worker movement, however, embraced the corporatist guild ideals that better fit the Christian social democratic milieu of Europe and its faith-based union associations.

The labor schools did not fit into the higher education apostolic ideal of the Society of Jesus, and the labor priests never received the same respect as their higher education counterparts. However, Father General Wlodimir Ledochowski, who had supervised the writing of *Quadragesimo Anno*, wanted to put flesh on the bones of the social magisterium. This apostolic work was one attempt among others to achieve Ledochowski's goal. Qualified Catholic laymen often taught in these schools because Jesuits tended to be too theoretical and churchy or the workingmen fell into a pattern of obsequious timidity with the clergy. Indeed, the Jesuits acted like parish priests within the social setting of labor unionism, always lending a sympathetic ear and a word of encouragement. In addition, they normally lectured on labor ethics to underline the balance between property and the workers' right to associate to better their lot.[6] The Xavier Labor School in Manhattan was the most famous of these institutions during this era, in part because of the power and influence of the New York City unions. The Jesuits Phillip Carey, SJ, and John Corridan, SJ, who was the priest portrayed in the movie *On the Water-front*, led the enterprise.[7] The school served unions from 1941 to 1989, and President John Sweeney of the AFL-CIO is an alumnus. The Boston Catholic Labor Guild, directed by Father Ed Boyle, SJ, is the only labor school left today.

Peter McDonough suggests that it was not so much the Church's social teachings nor the communist organizing that took hold of men's imaginations, but simply the fraternity and camaraderie that developed from ethnic, family, and patriotic ties nurtured through these apostolic efforts.[8] The schools combined forces with the Jesuits' Institute for Social Order to provide workingmen's retreats on weekends and family day retreats for married couples. The emphasis of the Jesuits, like the Catholic social justice crusaders John Ryan and Peter Deitz, focused on the family, which to this day the Church sees as the fundamental social unit in the world. They believed better wages, benefits, and working conditions would lead to better family life. The Jesuits did not promote a rush for power to transform the economic system, nor did the workers seem to have a desire for such an attempt; instead they advocated a sense of fairness within society. When laborers had a living wage, they could care for their families. The Jesuit attempts at promoting the labor movement from the family up, through the Institute for Social Order and their affiliated labor schools, had limited success because they did not confront the most powerful academic, political, economic, and media forces. Catholics and other social activists would only bring about significant change by engaging those who had power within society. Furthermore, the gains made in strong union contracts never benefited the great number of workers who did not belong to unions, particularly minorities and women. With time, the Jesuits and their lay colleagues lost their teaching roles to the educational programs developed by unions, and during the period of prosperity in the 1950s, the social justice aspect of the labor movement also came into question as union workers were living well.

During these years, the Jesuit labor priests openly admired communist organizers for their zeal and grappled with the apathy of Catholics for some non-communist attempts at social change. The emphasis on pastoral concerns in a secular context (e.g., the union hall) and a certain resignation to always having the poor at hand probably impeded further economic change on a grander scale.[9] The Jesuits were clearly not encouraging Catholic union members as a movement (e.g., like the budding civil rights movement) to confront the economic and political elites of the time in creating a new economic system. Economic change was not forthcoming because the Jesuit vision lacked a greater sense of urgency; moreover, the corporatism of *Quadragesimo Anno* was arcane to workers and even many labor priests.

In contrast, Monsignor John Ryan during the 1930s saw great hope in the corporatism of *Quadragesimo Anno* and promoted the National Industry Councils of the Roosevelt administration as vehicles to meld Pius XI's corporatism with the New Deal efforts to rebuild the economy. Ryan had promoted worker-ownership, worker management, and profit sharing since writing the Bishop's Plan for Social Reconstruction in 1919. Father Raymond McGowan, Ryan's assistant, had encouraged employer-labor-government conferences since the early 1920s.[10] The Jesuits and labor school priests, like managers and union members of the 1940s and 1950s, had settled into a zone of comfort with a transitional method of straightforward collective bargaining. To be sympathetic to progressive religious people who desired a more just economic system for all workers, Catholic union members who prospered during the 1940s and 1950s lost their passion to keep the changes of the New Deal moving. In other words, Catholics were climbing up the economic ladder and a certain sense of complacency had set in.

AFL-CIO in the 1950s

Despite the Taft-Hartley Act of 1947, workers continued to join union ranks and by the 1950s, one-third of the non-agricultural labor force was organized. President Truman used his presidential power to seek temporary injunctions against mine workers and steel workers as did Eisenhower with longshoremen.[11] Strike activity decreased after the passage of the Taft-Hartley Act, but labor continued to show its strength and role in the economy. During these early years of the Cold War, both the AFL and CIO took every means to prevent the spread of communism in foreign lands and within their own communities.[12] Labor leaders endorsed the Marshall Plan, encouraged foreign aid, and backed the United Nations in the Korean intervention.[13]

By the 1950s, the union movement had become an acceptable part of the American economic and political scene. The leaders often had better education than their own parents and grandparents, and they became peers with their management adversaries, albeit not social equals. The bureaucracy of the labor movement built an obstacle between unions and their members.[14] George Meany, president of the AFL, and Walter Reuther, the CIO president, came to terms on a no-raiding agreement in 1953.[15] By 1955, the two federations had agreed to a formal merger with George Meany as president and Walter Reuther as head of the Industrial Union Department. Leaders and journalists saw the merger as a means to prevent racketeering from destroying the credibility of labor, to create a unified position against communism, and to establish the goal of bringing any willing worker into the union ranks no matter color or creed.[16] Labor radicals also saw this merger as an end to the communist supported organizing drives of the CIO.

In spite of the benefits of a unified labor movement, the percentage of union members in the non-agricultural work force reached its apogee in 1955 at 35 percent.[17] The merger did not automatically produce organizing successes. Employers became more enlightened, providing better wages and working conditions to employees, and the South remained very much nonunion. How could attempts at greater democracy in the workplace find success in a region where civil rights were still denied? "In many instances the labor leaders themselves, both at the top and at local levels, appeared to have lost something of the zeal that had marked their organizing activity in the past."[18] The number of blue collar jobs dropped from 40.7 percent of the total labor force to 36.4 percent between 1947 and 1963. At the same time, white collar jobs increased from 45.3 percent to 57 percent.[19] White collar workers were less likely to join unions, and agricultural workers were not included in these statistics. On the political front, the Committee on Political Education (COPE) campaigned for Democratic candidates and lobbied for repeal of the Taft-Hartley Act.[20]

Corruption in the union movement was a desultory element for both employers and employees and had been present in some unions since the early part of the century. The building trades, longshoremen, truck drivers, and other service workers were more susceptible to this corruption because of the nature of their work and the employers' dependency on it. After prohibition, racketeering and organized crime made greater inroads into various unions, and the members, employers, and public became more concerned with the damage that could be done by unsavory figures in industrial relations. The AFL-CIO attempted to combat this problem with its Ethical Practices Committee which investigated charges of rigged union elections, the misappropriation of money, and illegal union activities.[21] The federal government also followed suit when the Senate established the Select Committee on Improper Activities in the Labor Management Field. The number of corrupt unions was small, but the public testimony and news reports cast a dark shadow on the entire labor movement. Republicans subsequently called for strict measures to eliminate corruption, so strict that Democrats saw the measures as an attempt to weaken the labor movement. The outcome of all the political wrangling was the Landrum-Griffin Act that was signed into law in 1959. The Landrum-Griffin Act created the means to protect employees and employers from unscrupulous labor leaders and organized crime, but it went further and weakened unions by making it illegal for a union to put almost any pressure on a secondary employer. It also prohibited a union from picketing employers who have recognized a lawful rival union and gave states greater rights in administering labor relations over labor disputes deemed insignificant by the NLRB.[22] The latter change made it harder for unions to organize in right-to-work states. Subsequent investigations under the auspices of the Landrum-Griffin Act showed union corruption to be much less widespread than had been previously believed, but the government had nonetheless usurped power in the industrial relations field.

During the 1960s and 1970s labor needed to build up its political clout with the general public to demand greater employment for all Americans; it nevertheless missed an opportunity to join with the civil rights movement to promote work in any society as a human right and not a privilege for the few. Also, labor and management began to submit more questions to arbitration, and industrial relations commentators argued that in the case of strikes affecting the entire nation a more refined system of judicial inquiry and fact finding should be developed—industrial jurisprudence. Over time, as seen by intellectuals on the left, the industrial relations and industrial jurisprudence model that developed became calcified when industrial pluralism (the pluralistic-democratic view of progressive labor) morphed into Big Labor as a special interest. Conservatives had already labeled unionized labor a special interest group, but the dwindling progressive efforts of unions and their focus on control of labor markets produced friction when politics turned to debates over "rights" for women, the aged, the physically challenged, minorities, and so on. "The unions," according to Nelson Lichtenstein, were now "Big Labor": in the 1950s and 1960s it seemed to many former allies that caution, bureaucracy, and self-interest had replaced the visionary quest for solidarity and social transformation that had been the hallmark of the depression decade."[23] Unions had become service centers to enforce contracts and negotiate new ones. In fact, the arbitration procedures built around collective bargaining agreements (to bring democracy and justice to the workplace) would become more cumbersome and less fruitful than pursuing "rights" cases with the Equal Employment Opportunity Commission (EEOC) and the Occupational Safety and Health Association (OSHA). Furthermore, since industrial relations in the United States have centered on individual firms and not entire industries, by the 1980s with only 16 percent of the workforce organized, there were 175,000 collective-bargaining agreements and 70,000 local unions. "The burdensome and decentralized union-servicing function meant that, whatever the politics or personalities of those who led individual unions, the time, money, and effort that went into organizing and internal education fell away sharply."[24]

George Meany was a conservative trade unionist who led the AFL-CIO in supporting the war in Vietnam. He moved slowly to end racial discrimination within the union movement because seniority was such a key element of worker protection. This conservatism led to a mutual animosity between organized labor and the left. On the one hand, the labor movement supported civil rights legislation as a body throughout the 1950s and 1960s; on the other hand, its own hiring hall practices and apprenticeship program were often discriminatory.[25] The AFL-CIO did not sanction the 1963 civil rights march on Washington, and it was Walter Reuther of the United Auto Workers (UAW), rather than George Meany, who took the podium with Martin Luther King, Jr. The UAW left the AFL-CIO in 1968, and the AFL-CIO lost a progressive voice in Reuther who wanted more aggressive efforts at organizing and greater involvement in the civil rights movement.[26] As time went on, George Meany criticized the unwillingness of rank and file members to ratify new labor contracts and argued that union leadership ought to have full authority in contract decisions. He even promoted voluntary arbitration to alleviate strikes. Clearly Meany did not see the AFL-CIO as a social movement although he was a staunch defender of the union movement in our nation.[27]

Rural Organizing and Urban Plant Closures

As big labor and big business settled into a comfortable relationship in the 1950s, farm workers and other low-skilled wage earners became the focus of interest for religious activists in subsequent decades. Vatican II, the religious vocational crisis, the civil rights movement, the Vietnam war, and other profound social events changed the nature of religious participation in the labor movement. As opposed to the years from the beginning of the century to the 1950s, religious professionals were no longer engaged in the labor movement in a systematic fashion. Labor priests and labor nuns responded to social justice issues (in particular, labor issues) in a much more individual and ad hoc fashion. Although labor leaders like George Meany supported civil rights, many liberals and religious professionals felt that his calls for change were too slow and too timid. Similarly, priests, brothers, and nuns who were social activists in earlier times (e.g., Reverend Charles Owen Rice of Pittsburgh) split with the AFL-CIO over the Vietnam war and U.S. military support of Nicaraguan contras. Big labor had become too identified with big business.

Monsignor George Higgins contended that after the great labor organizing of the 1930s and 1940s, institutional Catholicism played a diminished role in the labor movement because workers had gained union recognition.

He believed Church leaders correctly refrained from becoming involved in the technical details of contract negotiations or contract compliance. Religious progressives and union organizers had won their goal of union recognition for auto, steel, and transportation workers. The activism of labor priests and professional religious turned to those who still remained unorganized such as farm workers and garment workers. The U.S. Conference of Catholic Bishops aided the farm workers by insisting that U.S. growers accept the right of the workers to have union representation.[28] In a similar fashion, during the Farah Manufacturing and J. P. Stevens labor conflicts of the 1970s, the Church stood behind the workers' right to organize. Both Farah and J. P. Stevens, low-wage southern textile companies, refused to recognize the unions of their employees and committed unfair labor practices to avoid collective bargaining. During these two conflicts, sisters, priests, bishops and their religious councils encouraged the employers to bargain with workers' unions, offered their skills to mediate disputes, and asked other workers and congregations to support the workers.[29] With the farm workers and the garment workers, the Church often faced opposition from Catholic growers and Catholic textile executives, creating tension in local parishes and dioceses.[30]

Farm Workers

In California, the farm workers movement was the most evident labor organizing of the 1960s and 1970s. The leadership of César Chávez and Dolores Huerta linked labor and community organizing to the influence of organizers Saul Alinsky and Fred Ross. The organizing of the Industrial Areas Foundation had taken root in Los Angeles because East Los Angeles Mexican-Americans wanted to bring the dynamism of the farm worker effort to the urban setting. Ernie Cortes, a former United Farm Workers (UFW boycott leader from Texas), organized the United Neighborhood Organizations (UNO) with the help of Bishop Juan Arzube, Fathers Frank Colborn and Pedro Villarroya, and Sister Mary Beth Larkin. In a real way, the Catholic Church supported the farm worker and UNO organizing with contributions from the Campaign for Human Development.

Farm workers were and continue to be the most impoverished wage earners in the United States. During the Bracero program (Public Law 78) from 1954 to 1964, U.S. farm owners and agribusinesses employed thousands of Mexicans to work in their fields. The government sponsored program permitted the hiring of poor foreign workers and therefore blocked wage increases and benefits to native-born migrant workers. Latinos and other low-income workers faced the onslaught of even poorer job seekers from south of the border, who at least had minimum wages and benefits negotiated through the auspices of the Mexican government.[31] After lobbying from religious groups, including the Catholic Church, and independent government reports, the House of Representatives phased out the program in 1964. Freed from competing with foreign workers, U.S. farm workers then had an opportune moment to organize.

Although César Chávez learned about justice and injustice during his years as a child of migrant farm workers, and again as a young man who flirted with the lifestyle of *pachucos*, and then as a Navy enlisted man, Father Donald McDonnell was the one who taught him the Catholic Church's social teaching. The San Francisco Catholic Archdiocese assigned McDonnell to rural migrant ministry, and he met Chávez in San Jose, California's barrio "Sal Si Puede." McDonnell taught Chávez the history of farm worker organizing in California and shared the social encyclicals with him. In *Mater et Magistra* (1961) John XXIII spoke directly to agricultural workers:

> Nor may it be overlooked that in rural areas, as indeed in every productive sector, farmers should join together in fellowships, especially when the family itself works the farm. Indeed, it is proper for rural workers to have a sense of solidarity. They should strive jointly to set up mutual-aid societies and professional associations. All these are very necessary either to keep rural dwellers abreast of scientific and technical progress, or to protect the prices of goods produced by their labor. Besides, acting in this manner, farmers are put on the same footing in such fellowships. Finally, by acting thus, farmers will achieve an importance and influence in public affairs proportionate to their own role. For today it is unquestionably true that the solitary voice speaks, as they say, to the winds.[32]

In the early 1950s, Chávez also read works on Mahatma Gandhi and other spiritual leaders. He had learned personal values of care, nonviolence, and self-discipline from his mother and grandmother while growing up in Arizona, and the lives of St. Francis of Assisi and Gandhi echoed their voices.[33] McDonnell guided Chávez in the living out of his religious and social justice views by introducing the young Mexican worker to the methods of labor and civil rights activist Saul Alinsky and Fred Ross, an Industrial Areas Foundation (IAF) organizer in California. The IAF continues to organize communities across the United States and was the spearhead for the first living wage ordinance in the United States enacted by the city council of Baltimore, Maryland. Although Chávez attributed many UFW victories in California to the support of religious groups, Monsignor

George Higgins believes these triumphs came from Chávez's organizing ability. Chávez was first of all a community organizer:

> Indeed, for three years Chávez gathered the Mexican-Americans in Delano, a little town in the heart of the vineyard area, into a closely knit group. He established a credit union from which his farm workers could borrow the money so often needed to tide them over. His members also found that by banding together, they could pool their resources and buy things they needed at discount prices. In short, the Delano workers learned what outside union organizers had never been able to teach them. They learned the lesson of solidarity, and they practiced it daily in the affairs of their own association. After three years, they began asking the inevitable question: If unity could bring them cheaper automobile tires, why not better wages and working conditions as well?[34]

Chávez's community organizing work started with the Community Service Organization (CSO) in 1952. Under the guidance of Fred Ross, who had worked with Los Angeles Mexican-Americans to elect Edward Roybal to the city council in 1949, Chávez and his friends registered 6,000 Mexican-American voters in San Jose. The Republican central committee challenged the first time voters at the polls and accused Chávez of being a communist. In this first taste of civic conflict, Chávez learned that tension was necessary for change and that the poor in solidarity had to challenge institutional power.[35] The CSO and Chávez organized citizenship classes and registered voters during the anti-immigrant 1950s just as the IAF and its Active Citizenship Campaign have helped legal immigrants become citizens in the 1990s. He also established a service center to aid the local Hispanic population, and he became adept at one-on-one relationship building through the service center work. Chávez learned from Ross and Alinsky that the organizer needed to develop personal relationships with the local people before beginning to organize for change. Since few Mexican-Americans belonged to unions, practiced primarily a popular Catholicism, and had little power within the Church, institutional organizing as done in Chicago was futile. Mexican-American farm workers came together around family relations and personal contacts. The family was the basic social unit for organizing.[36] On the one hand, Fred Ross perfected house meetings as a means of organizing, and the Association of Community Organizations for Reform Now (ACORN) is the best example of a community organizing group that continues to work in this fashion. Alinsky, on the other hand, had always favored organizing around institutions. Both, however, were clear on the importance of developing personal relationships with those being organized and identifying leaders.

César Chávez spent a decade crisscrossing California and organizing CSO groups in Mexican-American communities. He founded organizations in Hanford, Madera, and Bakersfield while Fred Ross established groups in Salinas, San Bernardino, Stockton, and other California communities. Fred Ross discovered CSO organizer and future UFW leader Dolores Huerta in Stockton. Huerta, after being hired by Alinsky for the CSO, became the IAF's first woman organizer.[37] As house meetings brought in interested family members and friends, the organizers began to pick out leaders and discover the issues that angered the locals: poor housing, inadequate schools, discriminatory employment practices, the lack of sewers, and so on. The supporters in time held a convention to found the chapter, elect officers, set up committees for ongoing organizing, and vote on a plan of action.[38] CSO, with financial backing from the Schwartzhaupt Foundation and the AFL-CIO, registered 435,000 voters in the 1950s and 1960s.[39]

The crossover from community organizing to labor organizing came in 1958 when Ralph Helstein of the United Packing House Workers of America (UPHW) asked Alinsky for organizing assistance in Oxnard, California. Helstein had been an important figure in the organizing of Saul Alinsky's Back of the Yards Neighborhood Council in Chicago. His union had organized Oxnard lemon packing house workers, but the citrus growers had refused to bargain with local pickers and hired braceros at illegally low wages. Helstein believed he could repeat a Back of the Yards/Packing House Workers type of win for the farm workers if Chávez established a CSO group in Oxnard. The area's citrus industry would then be vertically organized. The UPHW gave the CSO $20,000 for Chávez's salary.[40] Chávez built the local CSO into a powerful organization and began to send members to the Farm Placement Service to seek work. CSO members documented the rejections while growers continued to hire braceros. Armed with the facts, the CSO leaders in time won the firing of the Farm Placement Service Director and gained hundreds of jobs for local people. In this economic justice fight, the Oxnard CSO initiated picker sit-down strikes, boycotted stores whose owners kowtowed to growers, picketed the Secretary of Labor James Mitchell, and marched through the streets behind the banner of Our Lady of Guadalupe.[41] The work of the Justice for Janitors movement and the Service Employees International Union (SEIU) in the 1990s mirrored these direct action tactics.

Within a year's time, however, all of the gains were lost. The national CSO did not allow Chávez to organize a union and without written contracts, growers went back to their old ways. Internal factions also divided the Oxnard CSO. Despite the fleeting success, Chávez, Dolores Huerta, and Fred Ross sensed that the time was right for a farm workers union.

Chávez knew, after working with the Packing House Union organizers, that the common union organizing methods would not succeed with farm laborers.[42] These workers had not experienced the organizing successes of Midwestern and Eastern blue collar manufacturing workers. They did not come out of the same neighborhood or ethnic community like the Chicago Packing house workers.

The CSO organizers learned to use Protestant and Catholic churches to find area leaders. In a more direct manner, Roman Catholic priests promoted a farm workers union by going to the AFL-CIO for assistance. Father Thomas McCullough, a migrant ministry priest, and Father Donald McDonnell with Dolores Huerta requested organizing help from the labor federation, and the leadership responded with the Agricultural Workers Organizing Committee (AWOC) and a former UAW organizer, Norman Smith. AWOC, led by Smith and then Al Green in 1961, engaged in many strikes in the years up to the founding of the United Farm Workers. Although Chávez wanted to lead the CSO into labor organizing, the leadership felt secure in its civic work and voted down the proposal in 1962.[43] During his CSO days, Chávez became a more focused reader, and he had read the biographies of John L. Lewis, Eugene Debs, and accounts of the Knights of Labor.[44] At this point Chávez decided to strike out on his own, with Huerta following shortly thereafter, and both of these organizers left CSO work at great financial cost to themselves. Chávez's CSO work had taught him the importance of power and his views echoed those of Lewis and Alinsky. Moreover, Chávez sounded like Reinhold Niebuhr in his Christian realism that acknowledged the importance of building power.

> I always have had, and I guess I always will have, a firm belief that if you muster enough power, you can move things, but it's all on the basis of power. Now I seldom like to go see my opponent unless I have some power over him. I'll wait if it takes all my life. And the only way you can generate power is by doing a lot of work.
>
> It is unfortunate that power is needed to get justice. That suggests a lot about the nature of man. And we also must guard against too much power, because power corrupts, but it was not one of our problems then.[45]

The UFW began as an association of workers (the Farm Workers Association) and not a union. The failures of past union efforts made the farm laborers hesitant to talk of unions and strikes. Chávez avoided this negative history by building a strong workers' organization before beginning to even think of making demands on growers. The association provided loans for members, a burial-insurance program, information on workers' rights, contact with local schools and hospitals, and a host of other services the workers sought. Chávez's experience with the CSO and his constant travels helped him build up support in the farm worker communities just as John L. Lewis gained influence with mine workers in his early traveling days as an AFL mine workers organizer. The personal contacts and relationship building led to the groundwork necessary to create a force that could match the growers' power in any future agriculture labor dispute.

Many church people aided Chávez in his work. Reverend Jim Drake of the California Migrant Ministry, a Protestant ecumenical group, became a key UFW organizer. Reverend Drake along with Chris Hartmire and Phil Farnham, two other Protestant ministers, had studied Reinhold Niebuhr's theology at Union Seminary in New York. Hartmire says Niebuhr's thought simply fit the farm worker movement.[46] Jim Drake would later work as the lead organizer with the Industrial Areas Foundation in Boston. In addition to theological support, the California Migrant Ministry provided financial support to the farm worker organizing.

After some early labor disputes that drew the National Farm Workers Association (NFWA) into the fray, a flower strike in McFarland and a rent strike in Porterville (both in California), the NFWA joined the 1965 grape workers' strike of the AWOC in Delano, California. Vineyard owners were paying Mexican braceros $1.40 per hour while Filipinos and Mexican-Americans received $1.25 and $1.10, respectively.[47] Although Chávez, Huerta, and the other organizers were more concerned about building up a strong foundation for this new worker association after receiving a request for support from the AWOC, the NFWA voted to strike. Not long after, Walter Reuther, president of the UAW, came to Delano to support the strikers and likened their effort to that of the militant UAW efforts in the 1930s.[48]

Reverend Victor Salandini of the San Diego Catholic Diocese had allowed the AWOC to use his church in El Centro for organizing meetings during the early 1960s. During the grape strike, he lobbied in Washington on behalf of the strikers and helped impede the hiring of braceros as strikebreakers.[49] The Reverends Keith Kenny and Arnold Meagher flew César Chávez over San Joaquin Valley grape fields to encourage the pickers to leave their jobs.[50] They were later criticized by Catholic bishops and growers for their involvement. The Committee of Religious Concern included Catholic, Protestant, and Jewish leaders who came to investigate the situation.[51] After being stood up by growers, the committee held a press conference supporting the strikers, calling for negotiations, and encouraging greater support from the AFL-CIO and all people of faith.[52] Jesuit Father Jim Vizzard, director of the Washington Office of the National Catholic Rural Life Conference and an instrumental force in ending the bracero program, released a statement that the Catholic Church should support the workers in the dispute. Bishop Aloysius J. Willinger, CSSR, of the Monterey-Fresno Diocese wrote a reply in the diocesan paper, *Central California Register*, arguing that the dispute as it pertained to Catholics was solely under the jurisdiction of the local diocesan bishop.[53] Willinger was sensitive to the influence of Catholic growers, and editorial writers in liberal and conservative Catholic periodicals (e.g., *Ave Maria* and *The Wanderer*, respectively) would argue back and forth throughout the dispute about the proper role of the Church.

César Chávez understood the culture of the Hispanic workers for whom he fought, and an important element was their Catholic faith. Although the farm workers included African-Americans, poor whites, and Arabs, the Filipinos and Mexicans were often Catholic. Chávez and the workers gained national attention with their march from Delano to Sacramento.

> The march was a tactic Chávez had used with the CSO during the Oxnard struggle. Besides its practical political value, the march was linked to the idea of sacrifice. In Chávez's words, "This was an excellent way of training ourselves to endure the long, long struggle. . . . This was a penance more than anything else—and it was quite a penance, because there was an awful lot of suffering involved in this pilgrimage, a great deal of pain." In the spirit of the Lenten season, the march became a religious pilgrimage. It was planned to end on Easter Sunday, covering 250 miles in twenty-five days.[54]

Religious people marched with the workers and they celebrated the Eucharist along the way, although sometimes traditionalist Catholics, complaining of such outdoor Masses, picketed the events. The marchers carried banners of Our Lady of Guadalupe and U.S. and Mexican flags, adding to the color and symbolism. The appearance of Our Lady of Guadalupe had been the central event in the evangelization of Mexico and struck at the core of the Mexican farm workers' religious experience.[55] With the help of college students and religious, the wider public became more aware of the struggle. Urban Chicanos became politicized, and they identified with the Latino farm laborers. The media responded to the real life drama that the growers and workers were acting out in the San Joaquin Valley.

César Chávez's use of hunger fasts caused antagonism with his family, UFW leaders who opposed its religious connotations, and with liberals who saw the act as too Roman Catholic.[56] Ed Chambers of the Industrial Areas Foundation says that during that time organizer Saul Alinsky believed that

fasting was an ineffective tactic.[57] But Chávez's fast during the 1968 Giu-
marra farms strike, after violence had erupted between farm workers and the
company, taught the strikers the importance of nonviolent action and aggressive boycotting. Coming out of the twenty-five day fast, Chávez painted
a picture of a struggle that pitted the rich against the poor, a struggle that required self-sacrifice and a commitment of body and spirit to justice.[58] The influence of Catholicism and Gandhi on Chávez's use of fasting is clear. He did
not engage in hunger strikes, which are attempts to solicit a response from an
opponent. One is making a demand. A fast is a means of personal and communal penance and purification, in effect denying oneself for the other. The
fast was a means of communicating one's convictions, according to Chávez:

> The fast is a very personal spiritual thing, and it's not done out of a reckless-
> ness . . . a desire to destroy myself, but it's done out of a deep conviction that
> we can communicate to people, either those who are for us or against us, faster
> and more effectively spiritually than we can in any other way.[59]

César Chávez's most successful fasts took the focus off him and placed it
on the injustices suffered by the poor he had organized. He was not making
demands on others; instead he was giving himself to the cause.

> The key term is giving, which again suggests the principle of sacrifice as a guid-
> ing force of action. Also, Chávez closely identified himself with other leaders
> who demonstrated the suffering/sacrifice principle by their life or death: Jesus
> Christ (nonviolent religious leader—martyred), Saint Francis of Assisi (non-
> violent religious leader—practiced extreme poverty and gentleness), Mahatma
> Gandhi (nonviolent civil leader—assassinated), and Robert Kennedy (politi-
> cal leader—assassinated).[60]

Self-sacrifice mirrors the role of the scapegoat or victim theory of social
leadership. In the Judeo-Christian tradition, the victim leads by example
(nonverbal communication) and as a victim, the leader has clearly practiced nonviolence.[61] The successful fasts also strengthened the resolve of
the workers; they showed more patience (nonviolence) and hope in their
ultimate success.[62]

The Catholic hierarchy played a significant role in bringing a resolution
to the ongoing grape boycott at the end of the 1960s. Monsignor George
Higgins had written a statement for the National Conference of Catholic
Bishops endorsing the grape boycott. The bishops, however, decided to ap-
point an ad hoc committee on farm labor to try to work as mediators in the
dispute rather than endorse the boycott. The committee included Bishops

Timothy Manning of Los Angeles, Hugh Donohoe of Fresno, Joseph Donnelly of Hartford, and Humberto Medieros of Brownsville. The labor community knew Bishop Donnelly as a labor priest active in supporting the right to organize, and farm worker activists knew Medieros for his pastoral outreach to farm workers in Texas and in northern states as they followed the harvests. Without much action from Manning and Donohoe in California, Donnelly, the chairman of the committee, worked with Higgins and then Monsignor Roger Mahony, the committee's secretary in California, to attempt to mediate the dispute.[63]

The committee found that some of the growers were willing to negotiate with the union. The work of the UFW and its nationwide boycott ultimately led to the historic settlement with twenty-nine major grape growers in Delano on July 29, 1970. The National Conference of Catholic Bishops and its five-member committee had brought the growers and the union together for a peaceful settlement after the strike and boycott proved the power of the organized workers and their movement. César Chávez praised the bishops for their contribution to the settlement.[64]

During the grape boycott, Catholic writer, Reverend Cletus Healy, SJ, among others, wrote that Alinsky was Chávez's mentor and that Alinsky clearly flirted with Marxism. Growers used Father Healy's pamphlet about the dispute to sully the reputations of both Chávez and Alinsky with Catholics. Although Alinsky was an indirect mentor to Chávez, it was Fred Ross who taught Chávez how to tap into his members' values of family and faith to meet power with power. Nothing suggests that communist plots and conspiracies were part of this organizing success. Chávez convinced antagonists in the 1950s that he was not a communist by requesting endorsements from local Catholic priests.[65] He found that the support of Catholic religious made it easier to defend against accusations of radicalism.

With the efforts of Governor Jerry Brown, Assemblyman Richard Alatorre,[66] Bishop Mahony[67] and others, the Agricultural Labor Relations Act (ALRA) became law in May 1975. Brown appointed Mahony the first chairman of the Agricultural Labor Relations Board (ALRB). The Teamsters and UFW would face off in farm worker elections, but UFW became the dominant bargaining representative with 198 contracts and 27,000 workers to the Teamsters 115 contracts and 12,000 workers. The ALRA became a momentary blessing. Within a year, the growers began efforts to enervate the ALRB mission to bring fairness and democracy to farm-labor relations. Higgins, author of *Organized Labor in the Church*, writes: "Within a year, the growers double-crossed the farm workers. They waged a campaign to weaken the legislation and, for all practical purposes, put the California

Agricultural Labor Relations Board out of business. The law and its one-sided administration have hampered the UFW ever since."[68] As with the National Labor Relations Board, conservative appointments have defeated the intent of the Act.

In addition, internal UFW disagreements over the union's direction and Chávez's dominating leadership also led to departures of proven organizers. César Chávez in the mid-1980s began to work on mass mailings and educational campaigns to inform the public of dangerous pesticide use in grape farming.[69] Organizing, however, was down, and the union had lost significant numbers of contracts and members. The institutionalization of agricultural labor law in California diminished the immediacy of the economic justice struggle and the wider public lost its sense of urgency. With the formalization of California labor policy, as with the National Labor Relations Act, the public and power institutions (e.g., churches) saw the labor question as solved. Over time, however, powerful hostile forces would neutralize the law's original intent. Jacques E. Levy, in his book *César Chávez: Autobiography of La Causa*, spoke of the farm workers movement as a communal movement. Levy contends that Chávez organized from a position of truth. He did not attempt to destroy the self and replace it with a community; instead, he sought the fulfillment of the self as it is found in the community. Chávez did not want Levy to write about him but to write about the union. "Chávez was opposed to having an intellectual write an 'autobiography' of him that would make him into a hero, but he recognized the importance that a narrative of the union could have in showing the spirit of collectivity. Levy worked with the farm workers as he wrote his book and Chávez accepted this textual representation." [70]

César Chávez was a person who saw a full integration of the personal and public self. For instance, Chávez felt that nonviolence required discipline. He recalled Gandhi's self-discipline:

> He had tremendous discipline, both personal and around him. He had all kinds of rules and insisted that they be obeyed. So a group of thirty, forty, or a hundred men at the most was very effective, because they worked like a symphony. They were totally loyal to him. He wouldn't put up with anybody being half-loyal or 90 percent loyal. It was 100 percent loyal or nothing at all.
>
> Then, of course, there were more personal things, the whole question of the spirit versus the body. He prepared himself for it by his diet, starving his body so that his spirit could overtake it, controlling the palate, then controlling the sex urge, then using all of his energies to do nothing but service. He was very tough with himself.[71]

He believed that truth eventually triumphs and that truth is God. While many Americans assumed they had a society of justice, family, respect, and fairness, Chávez and the UFW exposed an America of injustice (corporate greed and consumerism), divisions, disrespect, and relativism.[72] To achieve truth, Chávez fought for social justice and pragmatically used "traditional unionism" as a means to reach it. Although his pragmatism led him to organize for power, he knew society would ultimately need to pass to some plan of action for social cooperation. His plan was based on political power, struggle, and cooperative development:

> Once we have reached our goal [against the growers] and have farm workers protected by contracts, we must continue to keep our members involved. The only way is to continue struggling. It's just plateaus. We get a union. Then we want to struggle for something else. After contracts, we have to build more clinics and co-ops, and we've got to resolve the whole question of political action. We have to participate in the governing of towns and school boards. We have to make our influence felt everywhere and anywhere. Political power alone is not enough. Effective political power is never going to come, particularly to minority groups, unless they have economic power.
>
> I'm not advocating black capitalism or brown capitalism. What I'm suggesting [is] a cooperative movement. Power can come from credit in a capitalistic society, and credit in a society like ours means people. As soon as you're born, you're worth so much—not in money, but in the privilege to get in debt. And I think that's a powerful weapon. If you have a lot of people, then you have a lot of credit. The idea is to organize that power [of credit] and transfer it to something real.[73]

Authors Griswold del Castillo and Garcia comment on Chávez's Christian perspective in organizing and economic development:

> In this [culture of social justice], Chávez was closer to theologian Paul Tillich's *New Being* of love and faith and Reinhold Niebuhr's Christian Realism than to Marx, Castro, Lenin, or the utopian socialists. Chávez himself said: "I was convinced [that my ideology was] . . . very Christian. That's my interpretation. I don't think it was so much political or economic." This Christian democratic vagueness, strong in its appeal, was weak in guiding policy. A collective movement moves on the wheels of ideology, a pulsating vision or a need to implement a philosophical system, but for Chávez the conceptual system for a just society was not carried in the collective consciousness of a movement, but in the consciousness of each individual. The new society for Chávez resided in the heart of every man and woman as each practiced a life of sacrifice and charity. For Chávez, only a union in the pragmatic tradition of Samuel Gompers

(the nineteenth-century AFL organizer) could deliver "bread and butter" while giving people the opportunity collectively to sacrifice and commit themselves to a life of charity via union activity. Unfortunately, Chávez was not very clear on the direction that his union or the AFL-CIO should take.[74]

César Chávez and Dolores Huerta were clear links to the organizing activism of the 1930s because of their community organizing training and work under Fred Ross and Saul Alinsky. The United Farm Workers movement was the last great labor organizing campaign in California and for many labor activists in the United States. It galvanized workers, consumers, and students. Although the Justice for Janitors Campaigns of the 1980s and 1990s, led by many former UFW leaders, approached this intensity, the "movement" quality would not be achieved. John Sweeney in the 1990s returned to California to endorse the strawberry workers organizing in Watsonville and tried to capture some of the UFW charisma. Organized labor will attract other people of goodwill to the labor movement when they see the AFL-CIO helping to organize the poorest of workers. The UFW campaign of the 1970s brought together workers, unions, community groups, students, and people of faith, and Sweeney has sought this same mix for the entire labor movement in our present day.

In the 1970s and 1980s when the UFW was fighting for recognition with the growers and fighting off the Teamsters Union, the rest of labor was defending against plant closures and union busting efforts by major U.S. employers. In the 1980s, Los Angeles activists, often with little support from organized labor, strategized and protested with workers who faced plant shutdowns. This period of national deindustrialization is chronicled in Bluestone and Harrison's *The Deindustrialization of America: Plant Closings, Community Abandonment, and the Dismantling of Basic Industry* (1981). Corporate America had stopped reinvesting in new facilities and equipment in basic industries and had begun focusing on mergers, acquisitions, and foreign investments. During the 1970s the probability of a heavy manufacturing plant closing down in the United States was 30 percent, and these closings shed 650,000 workers, often union members.[75] (If retail closures and other ripple effects are included, Bluestone and Harrison estimate that 32 million workers lost their jobs during the deindustrialization period of the 1970s alone.)[76] Some community members and unionists fought back because they wanted to see employment and welfare built-up rather than torn down.

Other community members criticized union members who made too much money and enjoyed too many benefits. They sided with plant managers who complained of work rules that increased labor costs. At the beginning of the 1980s, steelworkers in Chicago made $40,000 per year when the median income was $24,000.[77] Heavy industry labor unions in the Midwest, the Northeast, and California had lived off the victories of the 1930s and 1940s and the social contract built between big unions and big business in the 1950s and 1960s. Union officials rightly contend that companies never failed to earn profits even during years of high wages, yet companies during the 1970s wanted the same high returns they earned during the post–World War II expansion of the 1940s, 1950s, and 1960s. In other words, maximum profit, not sufficient profit, was always the goal.

Despite popular opinion about the allure of the South, businesses also divested in the Sunbelt closing factories and at times moving out of the country.[78] The foreign competition of the 1970s and 1980s and management desires for higher profits changed the rules of post–Wagner Act/post–World War II labor relations. Capital had become so mobile (as a result of transportation and communication improvements) that neither unions nor local communities had the means to regulate business. Local governments began to focus on lowering business taxes and creating so-called business friendly environments out of the fear of losing jobs and tax revenue.

The time was ripe for a reaction from working people, but labor had lost its fighting spirit, and the general public saw big labor as another special interest group. Nonetheless, some people did respond to the injustices wrought on workers, families, and communities shaken by the closings and threats to close. Between 1978 and 1982, 18,000 union workers lost their jobs in Los Angeles with the closures of U.S. Steel, Ford, Max Factor, and Pabst Brewing plants. Around the state of California in 1980, 150 manufacturing plants closed leaving 37,000 people unemployed.[79]

Professor Gilda Haas, a Los Angeles community activist, relates that the Los Angeles area labor unions were not very militant during the plant closure years, including the United Auto Workers when the General Motors South Gate plant was closed in 1982. "The people who organized plant closing coalitions, to a large extent, were considered dissidents or leftists."[80] Much of the money to support activists who fought the closures came from religious sources.

> So here's a crisis. This can happen in any crisis. When there's a threat of a plant shutdown, you're going to lose your job, do you fight? Or do you hope that you're the person that's going to keep your job? If you rock the boat, do you make it worse? Or do you protect yourself? With that stuff, and in different situations, people in leadership [positions] or organizers stop people.
>
> It doesn't matter if it's a community organizer or a labor organizer. Depending on what kind of an institution you are, if you're an institution that's been

doing a lot of organizing over the past decade, which the UAW wasn't, in Los Angeles. There was a certain amount of complacency. All of the other shops had been organized for such a long time.

And actually, what happened was through religious funding sources—not the Catholic Church—Presbyterians, Methodists, and Episcopalians.[81]

The Los Angeles Coalition Against Plant Closures (LACAPS) activists did not receive much support from the Los Angeles County AFL-CIO Labor Council because the Council's leaders focused on the building trades. Mayor Tom Bradley had appointed Jim Wood, the Secretary-Treasurer of the Labor Council, to the Community Redevelopment Agency, and the building trades leaders naturally concentrated on the needs of their members. The downtown construction boom was fine for workers in trades, but no one in institutional labor was seriously standing up against the plant closures.[82] In three years of organizing with LACAPS, Reverend Dick Gillett, an Episcopalian who co-founded the organization, never had a meeting with Bill Robertson, president of the Los Angeles Labor Council.[83] At the same time Los Angeles community activists and workers organized against plant closures, other groups established nonprofit organizations for similar work around the state and nation.

LACAPS grew out of the community coalition that fought to keep the South Gate General Motors plant open. Reverend Gillett was the first professional religious leader to become actively involved in the work.

There was a coalition formed to stop plant closures. I was about the only religious representative in it. The coalition decided to sponsor a major conference on economic dislocation, and that conference took place in 1981. It involved sectors of the church throughout the West, and it was an international conference which brought people from Mexico and as far away as Canada. About 500 people came to the conference in Los Angeles. It was two days. It had 30 workshops, broad trade union participation, broad church participation, not the endorsement of the hierarchy of any church but grassroots Roman Catholics, Jews, Episcopalians, Protestants, and I was the director of that conference.[84]

You were the only religious representation?
[Only] in the GM coalition.

Why was there no other religious representation at the time? How were religious groups participating and not participating, and the reasons?
It just doesn't seem to be, at first glance, a religious issue. And at that time, too, in the early 1980s, the credibility of labor unions was very low, following

the history of labor unions, which were not only in decline since the early '70s but seemed to be for the most progressive church people irrelevant to the major struggles.

What were the other struggles of the church people?

Civil rights, the Vietnam war, the organizing of various sorts, various political issues such as open housing and that sort of thing. And those were the issues, including the farm workers, which attracted religious people. And I have my own take, which I guess many others do too, on the farm workers as an attraction to the churches. And the question can be asked, why are the churches attracted to, ally themselves with, the farm worker effort and not with other union efforts?

First of all, the farm worker effort was well organized and had a religious component. One has to say that, and it was very heavily in the public eye. But the churches—I think there was a certain romanticism to the churches, seeing themselves as alongside the struggling farm worker. It was easy to identify with the farm worker. It would be hard to identify with a white-collar worker in an auto plant who was making a lot of money, and it was going to close, and that auto worker could find work surely someplace.

And out of that General Motors coalition, there was a group called the Los Angeles Coalition Against Plant Shutdown, LACAPS, and LACAPS got funding from various churches. I have to confess, I can't remember where the elements—groups from the Catholic Church put money into it. But it had staff for two or three years.[85]

During these years LACAPS also worked with the UAW members who fought the closure of the General Motors Van Nuys plant. Various religious leaders participated in the struggle including Catholic Bishop Juan Arzube and Claretian Father Luis Olivares. The decade-long history of the community and labor efforts to keep the plant open is well-documented in Eric Mann's *Taking on General Motors: A Case Study of the UAW Campaign to Keep GM Van Nuys Open* (1987). In this case, the coalition and its organizing against General Motors prevented management from closing the plant much sooner than the company would have liked. This plant, however, ultimately closed in 1992 like all the others. Mann believes the campaign always had moral authority and the ethics were clear, but the workers and community leaders faltered on initiative, public support, and power. General Motors, attempting to neutralize the community/labor forces, tried to gain some moral authority by depicting the UAW and its members as people who would not work as a "team" with management.[86]

As the Catholic Church, community organizing, and labor organizing moved into the last decade of the twentieth century, the AFL-CIO leadership was engaged in a struggle to turn around the labor movement. The growing immigrant population in Los Angeles had also asserted its own power with worker-led strikes in the drywall industry, building maintenance, and at low-wage manufacturing plants. John Sweeney, the progressive president of SEIU, the country's fastest growing union, had become the leader of the AFL-CIO. Could the U.S. labor movement reestablish itself with a new zeal to organize new workers?

Notes

1. Melyvn Dubofsky and Foster Rhea Dulles, *Labor in America: A History*, 6th ed. (Wheeling, Ill.: Harlan Davidson, Inc., 1999), 310.

2. George Higgins, *Organized Labor in the Church*, with William Bole (New York: Paulist Press, 1993), 31.

3. Dubofsky and Dulles, *Labor in America*, 358.

4. Peter McDonough, *Men Astutely Trained: A History of the Jesuits in the American Century* (New York: The Free Press, 1994), 5.

5. Michael Engh, Rector Loyola Marymount University. Interview by author May 9, 1997, Los Angeles, Calif.

6. McDonough, 101.

7. John Sweeney, *America Needs a Raise*, with David Kusnet (New York: Houghton Mifflin Co., 1996), 14.

8. McDonough, 103.

9. Ibid., 116.

10. Higgins, 54.

11. Dubofsky and Dulles, 340–43.

12. Ibid., 346–47.

13. Ibid., 347.

14. Dubofsky and Dulles, 350.

15. Ibid., 351.

16. Ibid., 352.

17. Ibid., 355.

18. Ibid., 356.

19. Ibid., 357.

20. Ibid.

21. Ibid., 358.

22. Ibid., 362.

23. Nelson Lichtenstein, *The State of the Union: A Century of American Labor* (Princeton, N.J.: Princeton University Press, 2002), 142.

24. Ibid., 142–44.

25. Robert Zieger, "George Meany: Labor's Organization Man," in Melvyn Dubofsky and Warren Van Tine, *Labor Leaders in America* (Urbana: University of Illinois Press, 1987), 343.

26. Ibid., 342.

27. Ibid., 345.

28. Higgins, 63.

29. Patrick J. Sullivan, *Blue Collar-Roman Collar-White Collar: U.S. Catholic Involvement in Labor Management Controversies: 1960–1980* (Lanham, Md.: University Press of America, 1987), 200–58.

30. Ibid., 52 and 239–40.

31. Higgins, 85.

32. *Mater et Magistra* 1961, 146.

33. Richard Griswold del Castillo and Richard Garcia, *César Chávez: A Triumph of the Spirit* (Norman: University of Oklahoma Press, 1995), 23.

34. Higgins, 88.

35. Griswold del Castillo and Garcia, 26.

36. David Finks, *The Radical Vision of Saul Alinsky* (New York: Paulist Press, 1984), 63.

37. Ibid., 71.

38. Ibid., 63.

39. Carl Tjerandsen, *Education for Citizenship: A Foundation's Experience* (Santa Cruz, Calif.: Emil Schwartzhaupt Foundation), 87.

40. Finks, 171.

41. Griswold del Castillo and Garcia, 29.

42. Finks, 171.

43. Griswold del Castillo and Garcia, 33–34.

44. Jacques E. Levy, *César Chávez: Autobiography of La Causa* (New York: W. W. Norton & Co., 1975), 108.

45. Ibid., 109–10.

46. Chris Hartmire Interview 1998.

47. Griwold del Castillo and Garcia, 42.

48. Ibid., 50.

49. Sullivan, 43.

50. Ibid., 42.

51. Ibid., 45.

52. Ibid., 50.

53. Ibid., 52.

54. Griswold del Castillo and Garcia, 51.

55. See Allan Figueroa Deck, SJ, *The Second Wave: Hispanic Ministry and the Evangelization of Cultures* (New York: Paulist Press, 1989), 37.

56. Ibid., 85.

57. Ed Chambers Interview 1997.

58. Griswold del Castillo and Garcia, 87–88.

59. Levy, 465.

60. Paul Anthony Hribar, *The Social Fasts of César Chávez: A Critical Study of Nonverbal Communication, Nonviolence, and Public Opinion*, Ph.D. dissertation, University of Southern California, 1978, 295.

61. Ibid., 296.

62. Ibid., 297.

63. Higgins, 90–91.

64. Gerard E. Sherry, "Farm Workers Union, Growers Sign First Table Grape Contract," *NC New Service*, Apr. 2, 1970, Los Angeles: 22, in Sean Flanagan, "Catholic Social Principles and César Chávez: A Case Study," Master's Thesis, Loyola Marymount University, 1971.

65. Levy, 107.

66. Griswold del Castillo and Garcia, 129.

67. Higgins, 99.

68. Higgins, 100.

69. Griswold del Castillo and Garcia, 134–35.

70. Ibid., 107.

71. Levy, 92.

72. Griswold del Castillo and Garcia, 108.

73. Levy, 563–37.

74. Griswold del Castillo and Garcia, 110–11.

75. Barry Bluestone and Bennet Harrison, *The Deindustrialization of America: Plant Closing, Community Abandonment, and the Dismantling of Basic Industry* (Basic Books, New York, 1982), 9, 25.

76. Ibid., 26.

77. Ibid., 87.

78. Ibid., 31.

79. Ibid., 40.

80. Gilda Haas Interview, 1997.

81. Ibid.

82. Ibid.

83. Gillett Interview 1997.

84. Ibid.

85. Ibid.

86. Eric Mann, *Taking on General Motors: A Case Study of the UAW Campaign to Keep GM Van Nuys Open* (Los Angeles, Calif.: Institute of Industrial Relations Publications, 1987), 355.

CHAPTER SIX

A Swing to the Cultural Left Leaves the Catholic Church on the Sidelines

Culture and Labor Organizing

The labor movement in the United States continues to hemorrhage today. There are stories of courage and at times victories: the Justice for Janitors campaigns of the 1990s, the United Food and Commercial Workers Union (UFCW) and Industrial Areas Foundation (IAF) organizing of Hispanic meat packers in Omaha, the organizing of black and brown home health-care workers in Los Angeles by the Service Employees International Union (SEIU), and living wage ordinances across the United States. These successes, however, have not created the groundswell necessary to reverse the free fall in the standard of living of U.S. workers: immigrant and non-immigrant, Latino and non-Latino. While Latino immigrants might begin their U.S. work lives accepting low wages, no benefits, and poor working conditions, like the Irish, Italians, and Slovaks before them, they will organize to better their lives; moreover, their children and grandchildren will ultimately demand "more." Latinos have the self-interest to organize because they find themselves in need. Journalists and labor scholars continually point to the great success of labor organizing in Los Angeles during the 1990s as a testimony to this fact.[1]

The liberal "wouldn't it be great if" position does not work if there is no one who is willing to make the hard sacrifices to move us to a new form of socioeconomic commonweal. Such sacrifice requires an element of religious zeal that the progressive movement simply cannot muster without a moral authority that transcends the movement. Liberalism essentially has no commandments. It ultimately slips into a relativism that holds even liberal values and liberal pseudo-commandments relative. In the end, it can say nothing about what individuals should or should not do. Moreover, the progressive elements of American society would have to decide if any new economic order should be directed by a few elites such as those which failed under the coercive policies of the Eastern Bloc countries of the last century, or whether it would become an economic and political democracy verily based on the righteous will of the people. The second alternative that respects property and encourages individual enterprise is not incompatible with Catholic social teaching. It is based on the subsidiarity principle which introduces a division of tasks between institutions, corporatism which is the concertation of public policy with interest organizations, and a communitarian sensibility which advocates a collective way of living. At the core, however, Catholics, along with other religious-minded Americans, understand that the will of the people depends on being in a right relationship with God. Pope Pius XI argued in the social encyclical *Quadragesimo Anno* for a principle of subsidiarity in society that moves decision making and work to lower levels of institutions or bodies in situations where these lower and sometimes smaller bodies would be more effective. Again, family members should make the great majority of decisions that affect the family, not the state making decisions for the family.

The United States is unique because political democracy happened during an agrarian, pre-industrial moment in American history unlike in Europe where industrial capitalism was in full force as Europeans began to win their political freedom. For Europeans, political democracy necessarily meant some element of economic democracy in an industrial era, and the labor unions in Europe, even where their density is low as in France, continue to bargain for improvements across entire industries. Organized labor has a strong voice in the protection and development of the European workforce. During the period of rapid industrial development in the United States, Samuel Gompers and other conservative labor leaders encouraged a pragmatic unionism that kept radical agendas, both communist and socialist, at bay. (The Catholic Church was not alone in disavowing the proponents of Marxism.) Communists and other left-leaning activists were helpful in organizing workers, but their politics was never embraced by the rank and file to any significant degree. The United Mine Workers (UMW) President John L. Lewis is often quoted as saying that radicals were useful in organizing the great mass of industrial workers but that the hunter would always get the bird.

The American experience that fostered an immigrant mentality of working hard as an individual to get ahead might seem absurd to European workers, who are in fact cultural heirs of Catholic social teaching that argued for a more organic understanding of the relationship between individuals and society. Catholic Bishop Wilhelm Von Ketteler of Mainz, Germany (1811 to 1877) was instrumental in promoting a social Catholicism that responded to the social disorder caused by the industrial revolution in Europe. While he defended the Church's role in deciding moral matters, his sermons on the social question defended the right of working people to organize themselves to secure and protect their livelihood. Father Adolph Kolping, another German from the mid-1880s, founded journeymen societies to help workers with housing and vocational skills. Today, Kolping Houses are found around the globe. In the United States they once helped German immigrants find work but now they serve Filipinos, Latinos, and other more recent arrivals. Similarly, workers established Christian/labor/socialist trade organizations and political parties across Europe while all too often virulently atheistic communist activists in the United States checked any organic solidarity with religious-minded American workers. Europe's two millennia of Christianity softened the industrial era's division of classes with the promotion of a more formal corporatism. In Europe, labor has achieved gains and maintained its influence by supporting a social compact between capital, labor, and government.

For a short time, from the 1940s through the 1960s, the U.S. labor movement won higher wages, supported social mobility, and recognized American enterprise based on freedom and initiative. The labor movement accepted American capitalism because union members were winning a steady stream of "more" and living under a soft corporatism of pattern bargaining. Moreover, the great majority of Americans were not union members, and they had mixed feelings about organized labor given the power of some unions relative to elected political leadership, e.g., John L. Lewis' UMW as well as a suspicion of internal union corruption, misguided or not.

After the civil rights movement, the Vietnam war, and the Summer of Love, labor in its alliance with the Democratic Party found itself on the ideological left, which was foreign territory for many of its members, especially the Catholics. Catholic social teaching said much about "social justice" and a "family wage," but was relatively silent about race relations, loud and clear in its anti-communism, and absolute with regard to sexual morality. Labor found itself financing and getting-out-the-vote for politicians who supported abortion, championed affirmative action (which was unquestionably a two-edged sword for unionists), opposed American foreign policy, and argued for nondiscrimination against gays that has since become an acceptance of homosexual behavior. Although Catholic priests organized young Catholic workers in the Association of Catholic Trade Unionists to keep communist leadership out of the unions (for instance, Father Raymond Clancy of the Detroit Archdiocese during the late 1930s and 1940s),[2] a later generation of priests failed to recognize that as the labor movement began to lose power, it necessarily returned to allies on both the economic and cultural left albeit not card carrying communists. And today, once again, some of labor's most staunch allies at organizing have mixed motives. While economic development with a focus on human beings is common ground for good working relationships, progressive positions around abortion or same-sex marriage are inimical to Catholic teaching and loom too large in the world today to go without notice. There has been no strong Catholic voice in the labor movement to question alliances and positions that may alienate Catholic union members and Catholic supporters, and the death of nationally respected labor-priest Monsignor George Higgins has left a vacuum in labor's sensitivity to the Catholic conscience. Other believers, whether of different Christian denominations or religions, must also find themselves hesitant in supporting an institution that is now tacitly and implicitly taking such liberal positions on culture war issues that strike at the core of our communal lives. This comes at a great cost to labor even if labor fills the void with clergy from liberal denominations. It can be pragmatically asked if old-line Protestant clergy and their dwindling congregations can provide the appeal necessary to move culturally conservative working people, many of whom look to the evangelical and Pentecostal churches for moral guidance if not the Catholic Church. These very same workers may at times fail to live up to that guidance. This dissonance between labor's economic justice efforts and its somewhat quiet but evident ideologically left-leaning cultural positions will someday undoubtedly come to a head. The conflict over Senator John Kerry's reception of Holy Communion while promoting partial-birth abortion will inevitably place greater pressure on the union movement to permit members to have their voice heard when supporting candidates and advocating for public policy.

In *What's Next for Organized Labor?* Nelson Lichtenstein reminds us that culture wars existed in the 1930s, too, when huge numbers of workers of different races, ethnicities, and faiths joined industrial unions. On the one hand, the American Federation of Labor (AFL) was made up of a large number of Protestants who traced their skills to the labor establishment built on northern European roots. They belonged to fraternal organizations like the Masons, others had ties to evangelical churches, and all were commonly bond together as kith and kin. "In the early 1930s, when the whole social structure seemed on the verge of collapse, these plebeian elites had swung into the ambit of corporatist radicals like Huey Long, Upton Sinclair, and Father Coughlin, whose economic radicalism was matched by a profound social and cultural conservatism."[3] Conversely, the Congress of Industrial Organizations (CIO) organizers brought together radicals, Jews, African-Americans, Appalachian mountain people, and immigrant Catholics to organize the meatpacking, steel, and automobile companies. These efforts precipitated right-wing reactionary responses to organizing, red-baiting, AFL and CIO union raiding, employer-union machinations, and cultural fissures that at times would weaken solidarity. It was as difficult to organize in the 1930s as it is today. Lichtenstein maintains that success will only come when the idea of organizing captures the imagination of today's heterogeneous workforce and musters sufficient power and social legitimacy to promote its cause.[4]

On the one hand, Walter Reuther and Democratic liberals encouraged higher wages to create consumption that would spur economic growth; on the other hand, some students of economics counter that increases in productivity are always the key to economic growth, not wages. One might consider the growth in the last twenty years of Asian economies. Reuther clearly acknowledged his Keynesian sympathies in the now famous exchange with the Ford executive at the Brook Park Engine plant in 1952. The executive had pointed out new automated machinery and "taunted" Reuther by saying that the machines didn't pay union dues. Reuther's Keynesian-laden response was, "And not one of them buys new Ford cars either." In the case of autoworkers, productivity actually rose with both technological advances and employment increases until the 1970s. Then the flight of capital to low-wage, nonunion regions in the United States and abroad, and an inability to adapt quickly enough to globalization (i.e., lower priced imports) resulted in the loss of hundreds of thousands of autoworker jobs. It should be noted, however, that the downturn in the U.S. auto industry cannot be attributed solely to the presence of the UAW. Research has shown that organized worksites have traditionally had higher productivity than unorganized worksites in the same industry. And unions help reduce turnover, provide training, and support employee-employer cooperation and decision making.[5] Yet, no one denies that workers and their representatives can lose sight of the greater good in their short-term self-interested decision making. The AFL trade unionists—skilled workers—were slow to organize immigrant industrial workers, and organized industrial workers were slow to support ongoing organizing of the unorganized (e.g., farm workers), which means social activist religious, academics, and progressive journalists must acknowledge the non-egalitarian streak and apathy that runs through the rank and file.

The Irish-Catholic immigrants of the past are an interesting contrast with today's Latino-Catholic immigrants. While both Protestants and Catholics had emigrated to America since the colonial period forward, the first significant wave of Irish-Catholic immigrants to the United States came from Ireland in the 1840s as the potato famine ravaged the Irish countryside over multiple years. During the 1840s, a million Irish entered the United States, and during the 1850s historians estimate that close to 12 percent of the Irish population passed through America's ports. This Irish history is important to the history of the American Catholic Church because the Irish became the dominant Catholic ethnic group and leaders of the developing ecclesiastical bureaucracy. Of all the Catholics, they arrived first and had the advantage of speaking English. At that time peasants were pushed off their tenant lands by Irish gentry who preferred to pay the cost of shipping them abroad than being assessed for the poor on their lands.[6] The poverty found in parts of Latin America today and the migration of *campesinos* to Latin American cities and then abroad are a reminder of the forces of economic or social calamity that have always compelled people to emigrate out of desperation.

Charles Morris contends in *American Catholic* that Cardinal Paul Cullen of Ireland regimented the Irish church from 1849 to 1878 when he increased the number of churches and clergy throughout Ireland. Catholics in Ireland had not been participating in the faith, and increased Mass attendance and reception of the sacraments would only occur after Cullen's efforts at reform. Not only did he bring structure to the Irish church, his improvements in Catholic formation led the Irish peasantry away from its syncretism and immodest dance and music to a nationalistic Catholicism that more often focused its hostility on Protestantism than British rule. The purification of the Irish church and the massive immigration of its sons and daughters gave the Irish a missionary spirit, which led to the establishment of All Hollows seminary that would send 1200 priests overseas from 1842 to 1890. More than half came to the United States. By sheer numbers, the American Church took on an Irish flavor. German Catholics would come in large numbers to the United States in the 1870s and 1880s but they were still fewer than the Irish and spread out across the Midwest. Italians became the next significant Catholic immigrant population between 1900 and 1909 (approximately two million), and finally the Poles, Czechs, Slovaks, and Slovenians, all Catholic, emigrated in large numbers from 1900 to 1930.[7]

> By the 1860s, new generations of Irish emigrants were bringing the intense devotion to the Church, the acceptance of celibacy, and the deference to the clergy that Cullen had instilled at home. In addition, the unusually even bal-

ance of male and female Irish immigrants—Irish girls were preferred for household service—permitted Irish Catholics to marry more easily within their community than other immigrants, helping to preserve traditional marital and religious practices. Whatever the reason, Irish names account for nearly nine out of ten of the young men enrolled at the major American seminaries in the last part of the nineteenth century.[8]

The Irish mark on American Catholic culture is indubitable. Since 80 percent of Irish immigrants settled in cities, they brought their Catholicism into civic associations, trade unions, professional societies, and social service organizations.[9] Police forces and fire departments became wholly Irish. Working together, Irish workers organized on the job to improve their lot, and they counted on the support of the Church. Catholic Latinos have received similar help and long for more. The Irish succeeded in part because Irish religious took leadership roles in both the U.S. church and in U.S. cities, while Latino immigrants often have no English skills and clearly fewer Latino religious to serve them. American Catholics, especially faithful Spanish-speaking and non-Spanish-speaking laymen and women, can fill these lacunae by speaking the gospel language of love, that is, sharing their social, political, intellectual, and economic capital. Latino immigrants will respond. In addition to the language of compassion, Spanish as a second language has become a common if not absolute requirement for Catholic clergy. The development of Latinos will require cultural understanding. The Catholic Church remains a beacon of light to immigrants who often find themselves in difficult straits in a rough social sea.

Jesuit Father Allan Figueroa Deck spoke of the "schizophrenia" of the American Catholic Church at the close of the twentieth century with regard to the Hispanic population. While mainstream Catholics, especially progressives, were trying to create an egalitarian, democratic, women-advancing, individual-respecting American Catholic Church, Hispanics had different values and concerns that originated in their "Third World traditionalism."[10] In the traditional mind, relationships between people lead to stability and homogeneity not pluralism, order is established and behaviors determined as opposed to a culture of relativism where behaviors change with social and economic mobility.[11] This "schizophrenia" may be true for institutions that wish to engage Hispanics today, including labor unions. Once again the organizer's axiom of organizing people *where they are at* and not *where you want them to be* rings true. If the Catholic evangelization of Latino immigrants means lifting up their popular religion and not simply Americanizing their faith, then to achieve success labor organizing must also entail a respect for their values and a participation in their embedded social networks, families, and culture.

The Church evangelizes the gospel message while the labor movement evangelizes for worker solidarity; the two efforts are clearly not exclusive particularly when organizing Catholic Latinos at the workplace. Chapter Two attempts to show in summary fashion the link between the gospel and worklife. Catholics who are active in evangelization, according to Figueroa Deck, either evangelize around "spirituality, prayer, morality, and personal ethics" or instead focus on "sociopolitical commitment and action for justice." In fact, Catholics who evangelize Latinos should be evangelizing in *both* ways—"the evangelization of culture has much to do with structural change, and structural change has much to do with cultural transformation."[12] Like religious leaders, community and labor organizers need to acknowledge the importance of spiritual and religious development in a people and not rely solely on calls for structural change to motivate workers. Progressives who question the fragmentation of modern society, the idolatry of the individual, and the value of things over people would do well to remember that American culture can benefit by a reverse evangelization based on what some might dismiss as the old-fashioned values of Latino immigrants that are often based on religion and myth. A balance between individual conversion and efforts at social transformation is not foreign to the experience of American workers and labor officials. Aren't business agents at times working with members who have gone through family break-ups, struggled with addictions, or are anxiously searching for new meaning in their lives? The possibility of conversion resulting from an openness to the transcendent would seem to be a healthy step. In the past, some labor priests like their labor flock struggled with alcohol abuse, and one finds that Alcoholics Anonymous efforts would become a part of their pastoral activities at labor schools. It goes without saying that a nonliving wage, a lack of leisure time and benefits, and poor working conditions will not help men and women who are striving to be good spouses and parents. Unhealthy lives and actions are normally the result of unhealthy circumstances; in other words, efforts at sociopolitical action and justice are unquestionably a necessity. Spiritual conversion creates "the power and social legitimacy" necessary to cause change as in the cases of Dorothy Day, Mahatma Gandhi, Martin Luther King, Jr., and Cesár Chávez.

An uncritical embracing of everything that is American will not likely win over new recruits to the labor movement. Figueroa Deck reminds Catholics that an effective evangelizer (and perhaps a union "evangelizer" as well) must be at home in two cultures, his own and the one he is evangelizing. Yet he must remain critical of both. The gospel message has always been countercultural and transcultural, and the labor message must take a similar route. Potential union members will respond to calls to organize when they see organizing gives them what they like and when they realize that organizers know what they fear and that unions oppose what they hate. Potential members are pained by what hurts all decent workers, are pleased by leadership recommendations that they are asked to embrace, and are spurred on as recruits to do in fact what must be done. While the evangelizer/organizer has to become part of the culture that is being organized, a critical awareness of the transcultural and countercultural nature of the work necessitates maintaining a reflective distance from both the culture being organized and the culture from which he or she comes. For instance, no reflective union organizer in the United States would deny the strong individualism that permeates our culture. Figueroa Deck reminds his readers that the Catholic tradition offers a good antidote to our extreme individualism. The American labor movement might benefit from greater bridge building with the Church to leverage off its tradition of economic solidarity. He comments:

> The end result of North America's ontological individualism is an inability to live in solidarity. Indeed, the absence of the word solidarity in the sociopolitical and economic discourse of the U.S. is very telling. Its strong presence in the discourse of Catholic social doctrine is equally revealing. The Protestant notion that human happiness is the end result of independent agents pursuing their self-interest has never been embraced by Catholic social/ethical discourse. The corporatist idea harkening back to the middle ages has perdured despite the onslaught of bourgeois and capitalist ideology. Catholic social doctrine, then, is countercultural in that it makes the common good as much a norm of social morality as the individual good.[13]

He correctly argues that Catholic culture is not about upward mobility but about a downward mobility that works to serve those in need so they might live as true sons and daughters of God.[14] Those with more resources and talents serve those with fewer. He says a "critical cultural consciousness" is necessary with regards to U.S. Hispanics because Americans can too often see their culture as superior and the cultures of Latin America inferior. Similarly, Latin Americans living a subservient life in a dependent culture will also imagine their culture as inferior at times. Over time, as a consequence of a greater knowledge of the positive values of their cultures juxtaposed with an awareness of the oppressive history of their homelands, Latino immigrants and/or their children can develop a gibbering anti-American posture that fails to honor the positive characteristics of U.S. culture. Critical cultural consciousness is important for Catholics and unionists, immigrant or native-born, if they wish to support others with faith and reason.

It should go without saying that Catholic social teaching offers criticism of both left-leaning and right-promoting views of the social condition. In a sense, a Catholic worldview is an ideology that points out the chinks in Marxism and unfettered capitalism, although the Catholic view is admittedly long on negative criticisms and short on positive solutions that would assist unions and workers in creating a more just society.[15]

There are leaders who bring a strong understanding of faith into their organizing work: Ernie Cortes and Mike Clements of the Industrial Areas Foundation (IAF), Father John Baumann, SJ, at the Pacific Institute for Community Organizations (PICO), María Elena Durazo of UNITE HERE (a merging of the Union of Needletrades, Industrial and Textile Employees with the Hotel Employees and Restaurant Employees International Union), Baldemar Velasquez, president of the Farm Labor Organizing Committee (FLOC), and Kim Bobo, director of Interfaith Worker Justice (IWJ). While Protestant church disputes have led to multiple divisions and schisms, Catholics have customarily mediated differences and this requires patience. The IAF and PICO in particular do not take up single-issue causes because they are sensitive to the multiple views and values of their members. Unions need to learn from the success of this practice and not weaken their causes with alliances too close to the National Organization for Women (NOW), the gay rights movement, or other such single-issue efforts. Look at the participants. What is their primary interest? And then count the numbers. In California, there are 80,000 NOW members,[16] while the state has approximately 10 million Catholics and 1,071 parishes. Sheer numbers would suggest that maintaining neutrality on single-issues that are offensive to Catholics, especially to the Church's leaders, is probably a good strategy. Peter Skerry, *Mexican Americans: The Ambivalent Minority*, noticed the ambivalence that Mexican-Americans had with culture war issues in the support of Los Angeles County Supervisor Gloria Molina's political rise during the 1980s and early 1990s. She remains a supervisor and friend to labor to this day. Although her political success is undeniable, the mixed feelings about the source of her support bothered some of her own supporters. When she ran for the State Assembly in 1982, 70 percent of her campaign funds came from women and women's groups outside of her district.[17] Skerry observes:

> Such debts create particular problems for Molina. On a personal level many of the women who have worked with Molina express considerable uneasiness

with the views of the Anglo, particularly Jewish, feminists on whom they have depended heavily for support. These Chicanas point out that they could never bring themselves to join organizations like NOW. Indeed, they are reluctant to call themselves feminists. And with regard to abortion, they admit to serious reservations about the pro-choice position they publicly espouse. Summing up the differences these Chicanas see between themselves and their Anglo feminist allies, one Molina confidante states: "We don't hate our men."

Yet regardless of the personal views of the young Mexican-Americans who have rallied around Gloria Molina, they all understand that her outspoken advocacy of this and other such liberal causes puts her very much at odds with her socially conservative Mexican-American constituents. Thus, there is a definite connection between the stridency of Molina's positions on potentially volatile social issues and the quiescence of her constituents. Indeed, the latitude she has enjoyed to pursue what one of her staffers refers to as "elite issues" is premised on the passivity of those she presents.[18]

Gloria Molina's success has been heavily dependent on the support of youthful progressives who volunteer for her campaigns, which is true for living wage campaigns and other labor-related efforts as well. Skerry also maintains that California Hispanic politics continues to have the heavy influences of Marxist thought, leftist ideology, Brown Beret/Raza Unida activism, and academic/union militancy that was born of the protests of the 1960s. The Catholic Church was the recipient of the brunt of such political dramaturgy including the infamous protest of Cardinal James Francis McIntyre's Christmas Eve Mass in 1960. Members of *Católicos Por La Raza* disrupted the Mass after unsuccessful attempts to convince Cardinal McIntyre to use the Church's real estate holdings to finance barrio projects. These 1960s activists trumpeted Third World solidarity and revolution rather than reform which Skerry describes as much different than the political insider work of Mexican-American leaders in Texas politics.[19] The recent election of Antonio Villaraigosa as mayor of Los Angeles is a testament to the continued energy of this historically rooted activist power. Villaraigosa's past includes the leading of a Chicano movement "blowout" (i.e., a student protest) at Cathedral High School in the 1970s—unfortunately, the 30 percent voter turnout in Los Angeles' recent mayoral election diminishes any post-election cause to celebrate. One has to wonder if the transient nature of the Los Angeles population, which surely contributes to low voter turnout, provides the greatest advantage to the protest politics of the now fifty-something 1960s Chicano activists who have become the political elites of the Hispanic community of Los Angeles. Politicians on the left or the right will use low voter turnout to their advantage.

Family Values and the AFL-CIO

The Catholic unease with labor was born in the tumultuous 1960s when long-needed civil rights legislation spawned political identity politics that challenged a New Deal Democratic coalition which included working class Catholics. While communists were no longer a factor in the AFL-CIO, George Meany, a Catholic Democrat, was appalled at the development of "cultural radicalism" in the Democratic Party.[20] The cultural radicals supported the Equal Rights Amendment (ERA), promoted legitimization of homosexuality, and sought abortion on demand. While Catholics have always supported the well-being of women and children, Catholic social teaching based its living wage arguments on a single breadwinner who more often than not was seen as the husband and father. The Democratic Party was drifting away from traditional American family and values, and Meany did not know how to stop labor's slow drift in the same direction. For example, Meany did not support race conscious public policies but it became a demand within the Democratic Party. To preserve coalitions for labor's agenda, by 1979 the AFL-CIO as a body would support affirmative action. In similar fashion, while the AFL-CIO opposed the ERA, in time the federation began to move from equal pay for equal work to equal pay for comparable work. The feminist movement had entered into labor's consciousness, but unfortunately with time abortion rights, although still officially not endorsed by the federation, became acceptable social progressivism for some of the larger unions in the AFL-CIO. Max Green comments:

> As the old guard died off, labor abandoned nearly all its socially conservative views in favor of more "progressive" ones. The one partial exception so far has been abortion. The AFL never had a position on the issue, probably figuring that it was none of its business. Yet, as the composition of labor changed, as the percentage of women, many professing feminist beliefs, increased, and as the percentage of Catholics decreased, the AFL-CIO started edging toward a pro-choice position to improve relations with feminists. With that purpose in mind, it set up a committee to study the issue, with the expectation that it would recommend a pro-choice position. But when members heard of this, the sizeable numbers of union members with anti-abortion convictions—many, though not all of them, Catholic—lobbied the leadership not to take a position that violated their moral and religious values. The matter was tabled.
>
> Nonetheless, the executive council found other means of signaling that its views had changed. It took issue with the Supreme Court's ruling in Rust v. Sullivan (1992) that the government could prohibit health care workers at clinics from discussing abortion with clients. The AFL not only took the posi-

tion that the decision was wrong in denying access to information about this medical option but, in doing so, used language that indicated exactly where it stood. Speaking to the "broader rights" involved, it declared that its policy was to defer to judgments of the unions (most of the larger ones the American Federation of State, County, and Municipal Employees (AFSCME), the Service Employees, and the Food and Commercial Workers had, by now, come out in favor of choice) and to the membership, which had made it "clear that on reproductive issues they believed firmly in their right to act in accordance with their personal convictions" on what the AFL-CIO called, in the parlance of NOW and Planned Parenthood, "reproductive rights."[21]

Surveys have consistently shown Latinos to be less supportive of abortion than the general public even if Latinas undergo abortions at about the same rate as the general population. The Pew Hispanic Center discovered that over half of the registered Hispanic voters it surveyed in 2002 thought abortion should be illegal in "most cases" (31 percent) or "all" (24 percent) of the cases. Nevertheless a significant number (42 percent) favored access to abortion. Foreign-born Latinos who were registered voters also tended to hold more socially conservative views than their native-born counterparts. The Pew Hispanic Center found that Latino voters were mainly concerned about economics and education, that they would support expanded government services with higher taxes, but that they were quite conservative about family and sexual issues.[22] Abortion is a taboo in Mexican-American culture and when it occurs it is very seldom discussed. This unwillingness to discuss the subject may also explain the unwillingness of Latino leaders to enter public debates on an issue that has created a huge fissure in our society. Latino political leaders find themselves pressed to support the Democratic and progressive interest groups' pro-abortion stance. Up until this point, since Mexican-American constituents and pro-life advocates like the Catholic Church have failed to hold their Catholic Latino political leaders accountable on this issue, the politicians have finessed the controversy by remaining silent on abortion while letting their allies on the left spearhead the pro-abortion position.[23]

Along a host of culture war issues, Mexican-Americans have not been a monolith in their opinions and oftentimes Mexican-American political leaders have not reflected their rank and file views. Peter Skerry found during his research of multiple opinion surveys in the 1980s and 1990s that large numbers of Mexican-Americans were against busing, valued bilingualism but not at the cost of a solid education for their children, called for better control of the borders and restricted immigration, and did not endorse affirmative action at the same levels as African-Americans, who plainly have suffered from systematic discrimination in the United States in ways that Latinos have not. As early as 1989, the *Los Angeles Times* reported that 60 percent of Hispanics in Southern California felt that "[a]t the present time . . . there are too many immigrants in Southern California today."[24] Yet, more often than not, Latino political leadership is at odds with calls to restrict immigration from their Latino constituents. In the 1980s, many Latino voters were *against* calls for amnesty and *for* laws that sanctioned employers for hiring undocumented workers. Skerry reports that despite the Latino electorate's serious misgivings about further Latino immigration a full 78 percent of the Hispanic leaders at the 1984 Democratic convention were for amnesty and against employer sanctions.[25] Skerry goes on to say that this change only happened in the 1970s and 1980s because in the mid-1960s the majority of Mexican-American leaders wanted immigration limits. Today, Mexican-American politicians are in a quandary because the political ethos in the United States often forces them to represent the ethnicity and the minority group status of their people, but the electoral passivity of their constituents and the illegal status of other Latinos lead them to "rely on the resources of non-Mexican-American allies and sponsors." Inevitably, these allies and sponsors play a role, however indirect, in setting the Mexican-American political agenda.[26] This agenda can be at odds not only with the voters but also with Catholic teaching.

Latino politicians know that their community is growing but they also realize that many Latinos cannot vote. The Pew Hispanic Electorate report estimated that 60 percent of the Hispanics in the United States were not eligible voters in 2000. They were too young (one-third of Hispanics were under 18), they were too often immigrants without citizenship (at least nine million Hispanics), and only 57 percent of those eligible to vote in 2000 had registered.[27]

The culture war over same-sex marriage will continue to alienate many Catholics, not all, from fully embracing the labor movement's socio-political agenda. A recent example was the promotion of California Assembly Bill (AB) 19 that would have given gays the right to marry in the state. The list of supporters in the public analysis documents is revealing. The normal gay/lesbian groups are represented such as the Los Angeles Gay and Lesbian Center, the Lesbian, Gay, Bisexual, and Transgender (LGBT) Caucus (Democratic Party), the National Gay and Lesbian Task Force, California NOW, the Los Angeles AIDS Project, and so on. But the power of homosexual marriage supporters within the labor movement is quite revealing. Of the 203 institutional supporters of the legislation, twenty-two of them were affiliated with organized labor, some of which included: the AFSCME, the Asian Pacific American Labor Alliance (APALA), the AFL-CIO, the Los Angeles, California Federation of Teachers (CFT), the California Faculty Association (CFA), the Jewish Labor Committee (JLC), the San Francisco Labor Council (SFLC), the AFL-CIO Service Employees International Union (SEIU) Locals 99, 535, and 790, UNITE HERE, UNITE's Western States Regional Joint Board, and the United Teachers of Los Angeles (UTLA). There were *no* unions or labor advocacy groups that officially opposed AB 19 although one has to believe that many union members, not only in the labor movement as a whole but within the unions that endorsed the legislation, were of the opinion that marriage is for a man and a woman. The unions that supported AB 19 were among the most progressive in the labor movement and by and large public sector unions. In addition to the labor endorsers, a handful of Latino organizations embraced AB 19: *Centro Legal De La Raza, Instituto Laboral De La Raza,* and the Mexican-American Legal Defense and Education Fund (MALDEF). It is telling that the California Catholic Bishops Conference was a key institutional opponent to AB 19, and religious groups in general made up a majority of the opposition.[28] The bill failed to pass the Democratic-controlled assembly by four votes and every Republican in the assembly voted against it. Jim Sanders of the *Sacramento Bee* reported:

> Six of the Democrats who did not vote for AB 19 are Latino.
>
> The Traditional Values Coalition, a key opponent of the bill, said it targeted Latino lawmakers partly because of their propensity to be Catholics with strong family values.
>
> Persuading Latino communities to support gay marriage tends to be very difficult, much like "trying to debunk St. Patrick in Ireland—it isn't going to work," said the Reverend Lou Sheldon, head of the conservative group.[29]
>
> A California senate same-sex marriage bill did pass the senate and assembly in the fall of 2005. Governor Arnold Schwarzenegger subsequently vetoed it. The sponsors of the bill attributed its passage in the legislature to the lobbying of Latino legislators by leaders of the United Farmworkers Union.[30]

Gay issues have become a more prevalent part of labor's agenda since the mid-1990s. At the San Jose, California, conference of the United Association of Labor Educators (UALE), a group of academics and labor practitioners interested in promoting labor organizing, an avowed lesbian, labor instructor, and union activist asked the conference attendees to chant in unison, "Ten percent is not enough, recruit, recruit." She implied that in Australia, the gay community used the rallying cry because of the now widely disputed claim that as much as 10 percent of humanity is homosexual.[31] But she also was honestly promoting labor organizing as well because the organized private sector labor force was hovering at about 10 percent at that time.[32] The mixed message is symbolic, in any event, of the work and influence, the boring from within, of gay activists in the labor movement. In 2001, the University of Minnesota published *Out at Work: Building a Gay-Labor Alliance*. The book includes essays by the AFL-CIO president John Sweeney and Congressman Barney Frank. John Sweeney was instrumental in establishing Pride at Work, the gay caucus in the AFL-CIO, in 1998 although this did not happen without years of lobbying and two federation resolutions.[33] Both the AFSCME and the SEIU have had active gay caucuses since the late 1980s.[34] And Sweeney sponsored a sexual orientation resolution that passed at the AFL-CIO convention as far back as 1983.[35]

While the Catholic Church speaks out against homosexual relations—the Church sees homosexual acts as intrinsically disordered—disrespect and unjust discrimination toward homosexuals must be avoided. The Catechism of the Catholic Church states:

> 2357   Homosexuality refers to relations between men or between women who experience an exclusive or predominant sexual attraction toward persons of the same sex. It has taken a great variety of forms through the centuries and in different cultures. Its psychological genesis remains largely unexplained. Basing itself on Sacred Scripture, which presents homosexual acts as acts of grave depravity, tradition has always declared that "homosexual acts are intrinsically disordered." They are contrary to the natural law. They close the sexual act to the gift of life. They do not proceed from a genuine affective and sexual complementarity. Under no circumstance can they be approved.

> 2358   The number of men and women who have deep-seated homosexual tendencies is not negligible. This inclination, which is objectively disordered, constitutes for most of them a trial. They must be accepted with respect, compassion, and sensitivity. Every sign of unjust discrimination in their regard should be avoided. These persons are called to fulfill God's will in their lives and, if they are Christians, to unite to the sacrifice of the Lord's Cross the difficulties they may encounter from their condition.

> 2359   Homosexual persons are called to chastity. By the virtues of self-mastery that teach them inner freedom, at times by the support of the disinterested friendship, by prayer and sacramental grace, they can and should gradually and resolutely approach Christian perfection.[36]

In the case of homosexuality, the Pew Hispanic Center reported in its 2002 national survey that 72 percent of U.S. Hispanics believe homosexual sex is "unacceptable." The poll also showed Hispanics to have more conservative positions with regards to divorce than the general population. Prior to the 2004 presidential election, separate polls conducted in New York and Florida showed that low numbers of Hispanics support same-sex marriage. The poll in New York surveyed Latino Democrats and only 27 percent support same-sex marriage. In Florida, 20 percent of all Hispanics polled support same-sex marriage.[37] Hispanics in general do not favor homosexual behavior but at least follow a commonsensical line of thought that parallels the Catholic Church's position. On this issue, the labor movement has therefore stepped away from two natural allies—Hispanics and the Church—and has instead seemingly accepted the agenda of a relatively small but highly vocal gay activist community. The media during the 1970s and 1980s, reports Philip Jenkins in *The New Anti-Catholicism: The Last Acceptable Prejudice*, consistently took liberal positions on morality and gender even while the American public was supporting more culturally conservative causes.[38] This became magnified in the 1980s when some American Catholics, religious and lay, began to openly criticize the Church's hierarchy and in particular Catholic teaching on personal morality. The American priests who were receiving the most media exposure were not defending thoughtful, long held views of the faith tradition. In effect, the union movement had at hand fewer Catholic religious leaders—men and women—who spoke with a moral authority that transcended the immediate organizing battles. Either they were already halfway out of the religious life, openly hostile toward the hierarchical Church, or considered too culturally conservative for labor organizers and their intellectual advisors to find them appealing. This is not to deny the involvement of the relatively few Catholic vowed-religious and laity who actively support labor, for example, assisting with Interfaith Worker Justice based in Chicago and the group's local affiliates. But this involvement could be much more. Moreover, the media's portrayal of Catholic teaching on homosexuality as out of touch and the promotion of same-sex relationships by liberal clergy belie the public opinion polls that show a majority of Americans do not support such radical culture war causes.

The Catholic Church sees the family as the basic social unit of society, and a living wage is necessary for the preservation of the family. The complementarity of men and women leads to the ongoing establishment of families and God's gift of new life in the world, that is, procreation. Opposition to same-sex relations is supported on scriptural, philosophical, theological, and scientific grounds, according to numerous professionals with all the appropriate academic credentials.[39] Catholics have extended families, the parish, the universal Church, and solidarity with all men and women who are seen as sons and daughters of God. While divorce happens, premature deaths occur, and other unforeseen circumstances may reconstitute families, freedom and responsibility always lie in a respect for the basic building block of solid societies, a wife, a husband, and their children. The gay movement has gone from calls for an end of prejudice against gays to a call for a radical restructuring of the family that will never find acceptance in the Roman Catholic Church. This obviously impacts Catholic participation in labor's attempts at achieving economic and social well-being for all working men and women.

Just as communists attempted to bore from within the labor movement in the past, the gay advocates are boring from within today. Although no one condones the red baiting of an earlier time, Catholic leaders and Catholic union members necessarily had to defend their flock and unions from calls for class warfare and an ideology that promoted atheism. Gays inside and outside of the labor movement can be virulently anti-Catholic and anti-Christian. While groups that parody racial stereotypes in public often receive harsh criticism or official rebukes, the Sisters of Perpetual Indulgence, a group of transvestites in San Francisco, continues to mock the Eucharist and to stage perverted fashions shows with city permits in hand.

> Whether as individuals or organized groups, homosexuals have been among the most visible critics of Catholicism in the last three decades. Anti-Church hostility has been evident in the repeated lampooning of the Church in gay rights parades and demonstrations. The number of anti-clerical posters and mocking costumes indicates the centrality of anti-church and specifically anti-Catholic rhetoric in the contemporary gay movement.[40]

AFL-CIO President John Sweeney's article, "The Growing Alliance between Gay and Union Activists," provides a history of gay activism in the labor movement and chronicles his support of gays in the AFL-CIO beginning in the early 1980s. As early as 1982, John Perkins, the AFL-CIO Committee on Political Education (COPE) director, had attended the meeting of the Gertrude Stein Society of Lesbians, and in 1989 the AFL-CIO convention voted in favor of legislation to protect homosexuals.[41] Current AFL-CIO vice-president Linda Chavez-Thompson was a keynote speaker at the 1998 National Gay Lesbian Task force convention in Pittsburgh.[42] Sweeney, who is a Catholic and a member of the Common Ground Initiative, was in the best light arguing for a respect for gays and policies that prevent discrimination against gays. He mentioned labor's success at winning domestic partnership benefits and the AFL-CIO's support of the Employment Non-Discrimination Act (ENDA), which would prevent discrimination against gays in employment. While the U.S. Conference of Catholic Bishops has apparently not commented on ENDA, the bishops wrote an *amicus* brief in the case Boy Scouts of America and Monmouth Council, *Boy Scouts of America v. James Dale*. They argued for the respondent's right to terminate a leader who acted contrary to the institution's moral code, in other words, the dismissal of an active homosexual. Plainly, the Church neither promotes nor affirms homosexual behavior, and it will defend its First Amendment rights to maintain its moral view. Unfortunately, in the case of the AFL-CIO, some but not all unions and their leaders have crossed over from the position of protecting gays and lesbians from discrimination to advocating on their behalf for an acceptance of homosexual relationships. Sweeney writes, "Gay and lesbian workers were [historically] urging their unions to address their concerns through political and legislative avenues."[43] He goes on to encourage the building of a broad and diverse agenda by raising awareness of gay workplace issues, developing leadership in the gay and lesbian communities, building broad coalitions in part by "expanding efforts to build effective and long-lasting community coalitions and to encourage the participation of gay and lesbian organizations," pursuing legislative remedies, negotiating to protect worker rights, and restoring the right to organize.[44]

Dolores Huerta, the co-founder of the United Farm Workers UFW) and one of the most admired Latinas in U.S. labor history, caught her own UFW union members off guard in August 2004 by defending abortion and same-sex marriage at the UFW's annual convention. *Fresno Bee* columnist Juan Esparza Loera reports:

> Responding to Republican efforts to woo Latino votes by stressing conservative values, Huerta minced no words during her 16-minute speech in Spanish.
>
> "I'm the mother of 11 children, and I'm Catholic. But [abortion] is the proper choice for every woman. It's not the government's decision to determine how many children we are going to have," said Huerta, a couple of hours after Mass at the convention.
>
> Instead of the usual loud applause and shouts of "Sí" ("Yes") common at UFW conventions, there were only scattered voices of support. Huerta continued by slamming Republicans who cozy up to Latinos by defining marriage as only between a man and a woman.
>
> "Who cares if two men or two women get married?" asked Huerta, who is campaigning for Democratic presidential candidate John Kerry. "What matters most to us is how much money they'll spend for educating our children."[45]

The University of California at Los Angeles (UCLA) Labor Center announced a May 14, 2005 town hall meeting sponsored by California Assembly member Cindy Montanez and headlined by civil rights leader Dolores Huerta. Assembly members Mark Leno and Jackie Goldberg, former president of the United Teachers of Los Angeles, and others would participate in the "Latino Lesbian, Gay, Bisexual, and Transgender (LGBT) Community Dialogue on Civil Rights & Equal Protection." The event held at California State University Northridge, Department of Chicana/o Studies would discuss Assembly Bill 19 "The Religious Freedom and Civil Marriage Protection Act," with John Perez, director of Political Affairs from the United Food and Commercial Workers and the Democratic National Committee, serving as moderator. Despite the clear cultural division over the same-sex marriage issue in our society, a seamless link of organizing on behalf of gay marriage proponents exists in labor/Democratic Party/academic activist circles.[46] In May 2004, Milton Rosado, president of the Labor Council for Latin American Advancement (LCLAA), the Latino caucus of the AFL-CIO, joined Pride at Work to denounce House Joint Resolution 56, the Federal Marriage Amendment. The amendment would deny marriage to people of the same-sex, and the fear of LCLAA is the denial of domestic partner benefits. Rosado's press release reported that LCLAA "promotes civic participation, mobilizes workers to vote and works with national organizations to advocate for civil, economic, and human rights of Latino workers and their families."[47]

The relationship of the Catholic Church to labor and for that matter with the Democratic Party agenda will remain strained.

Notes

1. See Ruth Milkman and Kent Wong, "Organizing Immigrant Workers: Case Studies from Southern California," in Lowell Turner, Harry C. Katz, and Richard W. Hurd, eds. *Rekindling the Movement: Labor's Quest for Relevance in the 21st Century* (Ithaca, N.Y.: Cornell University Press, 2001). Milkman and Wong report on the successful Justice for Janitors Campaign in Los Angeles, and the organizing of drywall hangers in southern California. Both work groups were predominately immigrant and Latino.

2. Nelson Lichtenstein, *The Most Dangerous Man in Detroit: Walter Reuther and the Fate of American Labor* (New York: Basic Books, 1995), 188.

3. Nelson Lichtenstein, *What's Next for Organized Labor?* (New York: The Century Foundation Press 1999), 67.

4. Ibid., 68.

5. Richard Freeman and James Medoff, *What Do Unions Do?* (New York: Basic Books, 1984).

6. Charles R. Morris, *American Catholic: The Saints and Sinners Who Built America's Most Powerful Church* (New York: Random House, 1997), 36–50.

7. Ibid., 50.

8. Ibid., 51.

9. Ibid., 50.

10. Allan Figueroa Deck, SJ, *The Second Wave: Hispanic Ministry and the Evangelization of Cultures* (New York: Paulist Press, 1989), 7.

11. Ibid., 111.

12. Ibid., 94.

13. Ibid., 100.

14. Ibid., 100.

15. Ibid., 109.

16. National Organization for Women: California, http://canow.org/about/about.html (visited on May 16, 2005).

17. Peter Skerry, *Mexican Americans: The Ambivalent Minority* (Cambridge, Mass.: Harvard University Press, 1993), 246.

18. Ibid., 100.

19. Ibid., 256–57.

20. Max Green, *Epitaph for American Labor: How Union Leaders Lost Touch with America* (Washington, D.C.: The AEI Press, 1996), 118.

21. AFL-CIO Executive Council Statement on Reproductive Issues and Access to Medical Information as adopted at a meeting in Detroit, Mich., Nov. 9 and Nov. 14, 1991. As quoted in Max Green, 118.

22. "Latino Voters Most Likely to Identify as Democrats, But Party Loyalty is Shallow, and Political Views Defy Easy Categorization: Immigrants Transforming and Expanding the Hispanic Electorate," *Pew Hispanic Center*, Press Release, Oct. 3, 2002.

23. Peter Skerry, 278–79.

24. *Los Angeles Times Poll* No. 174 (February 1989), Question 21 as quoted in Peter Skerry, 302. See Skerry pages 300 to 304 for a thoroughly researched review of opinion surveys concerning immigration taken during the 1980s. While surveys often showed concern for the education of children, a significant number of Mexican-American respondents always reported that the amount of immigration was worrisome and that the United States needed immigration restrictions.

25. William C. Velásquez, memorandum to Board of Directors and Supporting Institutions (San Antonio, Tex.: Southwest Voter Registration Education Project, July 1, 1984), 2–3, as quoted in Peter Skerry, 306.

26. Peter Skerry, 311.

27. "The Latino Population and the Latino Electorate: The Numbers Differ," *Pew Hispanic Center and the Henry J. Kaiser Family Foundation*, http://pewhispanic.org/files/factsheets/5.pdf (visited May 24, 2005).

28. Assembly Committee on Judiciary, Dave Jones, Chair, *Civil Rights: Equal Marriage Rights*, AB 19 (Leno)—As Amended: Apr. 21, 2004, Date of Hearing: Apr. 26, 2005, http://www.leginfo.ca.gov/pub/bill/asm/ab_0001-0050/ab_19_cfa_20050425_134139_asm_comm.html (visited May 24, 2005).

29. Jim Sanders, "Gay marriage measure doomed by Democrats. Several vote 'no' or abstain as plan falls four votes shy on second try," *Sacramento Bee*, Jun. 3, 2005.

30. Miriam Pawel, " UFW: A Broken Contract (1 of 4), Farmworkers Reap Little as Union Strays From its Roots," *Los Angeles Times*, http://www.latimes.com/news/local/la-me-ufw8jan08,1,7202033.story?coll=la-headlines-california (visited Jan. 8, 2006).

31. Rosie Mestel, "The Kinsey effect: The Pioneering researcher's sexual revelations enlightened and shocked a nation. His legacy is controversial yet powerful," *Los Angeles Times*, Nov. 15, 2004, http://www.latimes.com/features/health/la-he-kinsey15nov15,0,6628508.story?coll=la-home-health (visited Jun. 2, 2005). Mestel reports that Alfred Kinsey's book *Sexual Behavior in the Human Male*, reported an inflated figure for the homosexual U.S. population—10 percent. Kinsey and his researchers did not conduct a national survey and interviewed prisoners who were more likely than the general population to engage in homosexual behavior. Reevaluation of his data and recent research data suggest that the percentage of the U.S. population that is actively homosexual is probably around 3 percent.

32. See Teresa Conrow, "Being a Lesbian Trade Unionist: The Intersection of Movements," in Kitty Drupat and Patrick McCreery, eds. (Minneapolis: University of Minnesota Press, 2001), 133. Conrow offers an account of the meeting I attended.

33. Kitty Krupat and Patrick McCreery, eds., *Out At Work: Building a Gay-Labor Alliance* (Minneapolis: University of Minnesota Press, 2001), xiv.

34. Kitty Krupat, "Out of Labor's Dark Age," *Out at Work: Building a Gay-Labor Alliance*, in Kitty Krupat and Patrick McCreery, eds. (Minneapolis: University of Minnesota Press, 2001), 16.

35. John J. Sweeney, "The Growing Alliance between Gay and Union Activists," in Kitty Krupat and Patrick McCreery, Eds., *Out At Work: Building a Gay-Labor Alliance* (Minneapolis: University of Minnesota Press, 2001), 24.

36. *Catechism of the Catholic Church*, 2nd ed. (Citta Del Vaticano: Libreria Editrice Vaticana, 1997), Numbers 2357–2359.

37. Eunice Moscoso, Cox News Service, "Hispanics Oppose Gay Marriage," *Hispanic News*, Mar. 24, 2004, http://www.hispanic.cc/hispanics_oppose_gay_marriage.htm (visited on May 24, 2005).

38. Philip Jenkins, *The New Anti-Catholicism: The Last Acceptable Prejudice* (Oxford: Oxford University Press, 2003), 53.

39. See Jeffrey Satinover, M.D., *Homosexuality and the Politics of Truth* (Grand Rapids, Mich.: Baker Books, 1996), and Christopher Wolfe, *Homosexuality and American Public Life* (Dallas, Tex.: Spence Publishing Co., 1999).

40. Ibid., 98–99.

41. Max Green, 119.

42. "This Is Not Your Father's Union," *Conservative News Service*, Feb. 8, 1999.

43. John J. Sweeney, "The Growing Alliance between Gay and Union Activists, in Kitty Krupat and Patrick McCreery, eds., *Out At Work: Building a Gay-Labor Alliance* (Minneapolis: University of Minnesota Press, 2001), 28.

44. Ibid., 28–29.

45. Juan Esparza Loera, "Huerta leaves UFW speechless," *Fresno Bee*, Sept. 20, 2004, http://www.fresnobee.com/columnists/esparza/story/9171776p-10071249c.html (visited on June 2, 2005).

46. Latino LGBT Community Dialogue on Civil Rights and Equal Protection, LALS listserv announcement, http://listserv.sscnet.ucla.edu/archives/la-labor.html (May 2005).

47. Milton Rosado, "Latino Working families oppose proposed changes to the Constitution," Labor Council for Latin American Advancement, Press Release, May 12, 2004.

CHAPTER SEVEN

~

A Need for Change

Reducing the Barriers Against Organizing— Can the AFL-CIO Revitalize Itself?

AFL-CIO leaders have estimated that every twenty-three minutes in the United States a worker is fired for attempting to start a union or protect his or her right to be a union member. In an employment-at-will economic world, all workers, whether Hispanic or non-Hispanic, necessarily know the power employers hold over them. Despite their past failures at bringing about labor law reform, union leaders realize that present labor laws fail to adequately protect workers who attempt to organize. To remedy this situation, in April 2005 a bipartisan coalition introduced the Employee Free Choice Act (S. 842 and H.R. 1896) which will assist workers in exercising their right to associate and organize. As in Canada union recognition would simply require a majority of the bargaining unit to sign union authorization cards. The workers would not face a protracted election campaign period nor need to vote in what may seem to be a hostile environment in their own workplace on their election day. The Employee Free Choice Act gives the National Labor Relations Board (NLRB) the authority to determine the language for authorization cards and the procedure for verifying the authorization.

The Act would also establish a first contract mediation and arbitration process. If the union and the employer cannot reach a contract agreement within ninety days of the start of their bargaining meetings, either party can refer the impasse to the Federal Mediation and Conciliation Service. After thirty days of mediation, if no agreement is reached, then the contract dispute would go to arbitration for an arbitrator's judgment. The parties are free to negotiate the aforementioned time periods and come to their own agreement on these periods.

In addition, the Act would increase penalties against employers who interfere with their employees' right to associate and bargain collectively. The NLRB would have the power to seek injunctions against employers who unjustly harass or discriminate against employees who support the union organizing campaign or first contract efforts. The courts would have the power to grant temporary restraining orders. Employers would face treble back pay awards if they are found violating the rights of their employees. They could also face fines of $20,000 for blatant violations of the Act during organizing drives and first contract negotiations.[1]

The federal government would protect the workers' right to association and freedom of speech at the work site regardless of their immigration status. Employers would not have the option of hiring undocumented workers and then summarily firing them when they attempt to improve their lot. The Employee Free Choice Act will unlikely become law during a Republican administration and the possibility of its passage during a Democratic administration is also doubtful. President Jimmy Carter was unable to win labor law reform during his years in office, and President Bill Clinton failed at achieving reform of striker replacement laws during his two terms as president. To succeed, labor law reform has to become a national call for change, and despite polls suggesting close to sixty million workers in the United States are favorably disposed toward unions, no groundswell for reform appears on the horizon. Perhaps American workers prefer the fleshpots and bread that they now have. Moses told the Pharaoh that he was taking the Israelites into the desert to worship God, but he said nothing about a promised land. Worshiping God is still our obligation as it leads to social guidelines (e.g., commandments, the moral framing of our lives). American workers today will not find a promised land of meaningful work and economic security without these proven steps—the worship of God and a moral life framed by this worship—no matter the form this faith awakening might take in our own day and time. Hostile employers and labor laws that limit union activity while allowing anti-union efforts, globalization, and fierce market competition all stymie workplace democracy.

Unions could possibly gain more than a foothold in the American economy if they had the backing of government legislation protecting the right to organize as well as to use secondary boycotts and hot cargo tactics. Secondary boycotts would allow workers and supporters to picket distributors and resellers of goods produced by employers involved in labor disputes (e.g., retailers not directly involved in the conflict). Similarly, unionists and their sympathizers could refuse to transport or handle the "hot cargo" of employers who engaged in unfair labor practices. These tactics would balance power by permitting labor to influence customers and distributors dependent on the employer's goods and services. But this means convincing the electorate that unions and their members are positive sources of economic development and communal well-being. The public will not support an organization of workers that strong-arms employers. Government support of labor organizing alone will not garner the support of union members and potential union members. What does a union contribute to the creation of wealth and healthy communities that is not already done by the employer and the employer's employees? The labor movement did bring Americans the forty-hour workweek, two-day weekends, retirement plans, and health benefits. Could it bring U.S. workers an even shorter workweek with higher employment as a consequence? How can it frame its cause as one that benefits all Americans and not slip into an activism bent around culturally divisive issues.

On the one hand, some unions need to have industry-wide bargaining power to survive. The merger of the Union of Needletrades, Industrial and Textile Employees (UNITE) and the Hotel Employees and Restaurant Employees International Union (HERE) into UNITE HERE is one example. UNITE HERE is attempting to obtain a single date to negotiate new contract agreements at big city hotels nationwide. The leadership will not simply shut down hotels in one city to reach contract agreements but shut them down in cities across the United States if necessary. The problem with industry-wide bargaining and centralized administration is less union democracy. The local membership's democratic prerogative has often led to conflicts with international unions especially when international unions place local unions in receivership, that is, under appointed union officials rather than democratically elected leaders. Industry-wide bargaining has helped the European labor movement maintain its political and economic power. In some European countries, minimum collective bargaining agreements are extended to nonunion workers in the same industry.[2] And this might be the greatest boon to nonunion service workers who have limited skills. Moreover, hotel workers organized in the biggest hotels can only push so far given that many unemployed and semi-employed people can learn their jobs in a short time. On the other hand, in an era when highly skilled workers no longer see themselves identified by industry but by occupation, the labor movement must more flexibly define the characteristics of its membership. People may not identify with an industry or company but with an occupation. Labor unions can organize self-employed men and women, private contract labor, and the un-employed, but this requires a unity of socioeconomic purpose that is appar-ently absent in the American scene.

AFL-CIO Split: The Change to Win Coalition

The New Unity Partnership (NUP) formed in 2003 was the forerunner to the Change to Win Federation of unions that bolted from the AFL-CIO in July 2005. The affiliation and disaffiliation of unions from the AFL-CIO is not unusual and the United Mine Workers of America (UMWA), the United Auto Workers (UAW), the International Brotherhood of Teamsters, and the United Brotherhood of Carpenters Union (UBC) have left and then rejoined the federation at different times in the past. In fact, in a sim-ilar move to rejuvenate the labor movement, the UAW led by Walter Reuther left the AFL-CIO and formed the American Labor Alliance (ALA) in 1968 as an alternative to a less than progressive AFL-CIO. The Alliance only survived for a short time. The New Unity Partnership had few ideas that were significantly different from the work already begun in the AFL-CIO under President John Sweeney to make the number one priority or-ganizing and training members. Labor commentators and bloggers criticized five union presidents—Andy Stern of the Service Employees International Union (SEIU), John Whilhelm (HERE), Bruce Raynor (UNITE), Terence O'Sullivan (Laborers Union), and Doug McCarron (UBC)—for initiating a new labor "unity" while embracing management-speak—"density," "market share," and "growth." The union presidents trumpeted their activist/mili-tant union credentials although McCarron had been known more for his or-ganizing efforts than any interest in social activism.[3] NUP's dream was to consolidate unions along industry lines and then grow the membership of these industry-wide unions across employers. Service work, transportation, and construction were all examples of sectors that would have consolidated mega-unions by sector. In effect, the union leaders portrayed their unions and leadership as the source of labor skills and social capital necessary for workers and employers in the national economy, and they intended to rep-resent significant numbers of workers by sector. But their implicit call for managerial rationalization, efficiencies of scale, and greater collective bar-gaining leverage through the consolidation of unions would inevitably lead to less democratization of the unions, placing more power in the hands of the international union officers and their staffs.[4]

The unions obviously need greater effectiveness and efficiency to survive, but trade-offs exist. Over time, unions have rightfully become increasingly sensitive to the multiple concerns of their members—health, safety, education, and civil rights—but these sensitivities can make them slow to respond to the exigencies of market demands. Organizational democracy provides a voice to members but it can hold back institutional action. The goal is greater union density in industries to wield enough power to influence wages and working conditions, which means coordinated and consolidated power in the hands of fewer people—more power to act, less union democracy. The leaders calling for greater consolidation both in 2003 and today are well aware that without "density," union workers are ultimately powerless. New Unity Partnership also advocated for fewer but stronger Central Labor Councils run by chief executives with weaker roles for Central Labor Council presidents, the goal being greater organizing success with fewer independently organized and administered labor councils.

Joann Wypijewski, former editor of *The Nation* but writing for *Counterpunch*, wonders why the New Unity Partners, who are now the Change to Win leaders, want to separate their unions from the AFL-CIO. Three of the leaders—Stern, O'Sullivan, and Raynor—were all potential successors to President John Sweeney. The AFL-CIO had followed the lead of these immigrant-dominated unions and as a national voice for working people it called for immigration reform that would protect its members and their families. The federation had financed and coordinated HERE's Immigrant Workers Freedom Ride and made the organizing of Cintas, the nation's largest uniform supplier, a priority supported by the Teamsters and UNITE's organizing campaigns. The AFL-CIO also orchestrated the Employee Free Choice campaign for the reform of labor law. New Unity Partnership did not, and Change to Win does not, offer America's workers anything the AFL-CIO hasn't already attempted. Wypijewski also observes that these progressive unions are really run by white, middle-class, educated outsiders, not the workers. She writes, "Stern's tenure as SEIU president has been marked by the creation of giant locals, statewide locals, multi-state locals, locals that belong less to the workers than the staffs."[5]

Change to Win unions have no answer to the loss of manufacturing jobs and now service jobs (e.g., call centers) to workers abroad. They have no ideas that are any different from the AFL-CIO's ideas with regard to globalization. These unions have continued to organize and maintain some strength because the workers that are organized in state governments, at hotels and restaurants, and on construction sites have one significant advantage over other workers—their jobs are not easily moved to low-wage countries. It must be asked if Change to Win's zealous leaders and organizers, primarily heirs of the social activism of the 1960s, can animate the great body of American workers who are more and more contingent workers, part-time workers, or casual workers. Even if union density were to increase, workers might not benefit from the corresponding bargaining power their union leaders gain. Some industries in Mexico have high union density—the unions are virtual cartels—but the members have very little to show for their membership. Change to Win unions operate by top down organizing with more success than other U.S. unions. Many of the people they organize have limited income, are pressed for time, and are happy when they can see their families. Can Change to Win unions become the social agents needed to right labor's ship in the United States? Are they a catalyst for a vibrant union movement? In the case of SEIU, the public sector employees and health care workers who have become part of the Purple Wave (SEIU activists known for their ubiquitous purple union hats and t-shirts) work for captive employers who cannot move south of the border to escape collective bargaining. Even in the case of hospitals, nursing homes, and home care services labor costs are ultimately born by the taxpayer. Should these workers have decent work lives? Yes, of course. But whether the success of Change to Win in these unique work settings will reignite the U.S. labor movement is another question.

The great surge of CIO organizing in the 1930s occurred after years of setting the legal and social groundwork necessary for massive organizing and increases in union membership. Wypijewski correctly argues that in many ways the workers were already tied together in social relationships prior to their union activism.

> It took at least fifty years for workers to figure out industrial organizing. When it finally had lift-off it was a part of a mass movement. In the meantime locals [union locals] developed, as the name implies, locally, through a combination of job actions, mutual aid, cultural activities, political education, party activity, target practice, newspapers, picnics, the warp and woof of life.[6] [And I would argue churches.]

Community organizing groups like the Association of Community Organizations for Reform Now (ACORN), Pacific Institute for Community Organizations (PICO), Industrial Areas Foundation (IAF), and advocacy groups like the Institute of Popular Education of Southern California (IDEPSCA), the Coalition for Humane Immigrant Rights of Los Angeles (CHIRLA), the Coalition of Immigrant Worker Advocates (CIWA), and UCLA Downtown Labor Center all offer training, education, and organizing opportunities. Immigrant populations by and large haven't embraced them as the vehicles for broad based change in their socioeconomic well-being or that of the U.S. population in general. In defense of all these groups that act as mediating institutions for millions of people, most low-income Latinos, especially immigrants, are working hard to maintain their individual lives. They are under stress. So the community organizing and advocacy groups leverage off of informal communal associations, soccer clubs, family networks, local teacher-parent groups, churches, and cultural centers for their work. SEIU and UNITE HERE are better than other unions in garnering support in these community groups, but the organizers and their intellectual advisors also put into play their own questionable cultural agendas. This may not only alienate at least some of the would-be followers, for example members of Pentecostal, Evangelical, and Fundamentalist churches with strong religious values and practices, but it may also ultimately create cooler responses from the Catholic Church. For instance, is the Pride at Work, Southern California organization (PAW) with its small membership that promotes a gay lifestyle more likely to jump-start economic organizing and labor outreach in the region or is the Catholic Church with 4.5 million Catholics? Gay caucuses in the region's labor unions are concentrated in the National Education Association (NEA), the American Federation of Teachers (AFT), the American Federation of State, County, and Municipal Employees (AFSCME), the Service Employees International Union (SEIU), the United Food and Commercial Workers International Union (UFCW), and the Communications Workers of America (CWA), the most culturally liberal of unions. It is hard to imagine Pride at Work building significant bridges between unions and the Hispanic community as any attempts will always be strained.

Righting the Labor Movement

Like religious-minded people and organized bodies of people in all places and all times, supporters of the labor movement have a fundamental need for conversion. This requires individuals doing good and avoiding evil while working communally with others who are doing good and avoiding evil as a society. Mahatma Gandhi, Martin Luther King, Jr., and César Chávez knew this so very well. In the perspective of reflective Catholic thinkers, the labor movement at this point in history is like so much of our wider society and has entered into an irreligious, secular way of proceeding. Chapter Two suggests that for work to have meaning people need to link their efforts to the transcendent—God. The least practicing person of faith knows that human beings work to care for themselves and those they love and that their efforts are tied to being God's children. Through such awareness one discovers moral truths that help a person live a good and happy life despite any obstacles he or she might face. The Catholic Church has discovered with time that humanity's procreative and human nature is never disconnected from God's creative force. Remarkably, while atheist Sigmund Freud is championed for recognizing the importance and power of sexuality in people's lives, the Catholic Church is denigrated for recognizing the same truth and, moreover, teaching that everyone has a responsibility to each other and to God in living out this basic element of life.[7] In the eyes of many observers, the attack on the family in U.S. society has done more to destroy the labor movement than any weakening of the National Labor Relations Act (NLRA). When labor unions, primarily the leaders, advisors and staff, begin to link themselves with pro-abortion and pro-homosexuality groups, they contribute to the demise of the family which is society's building block.

Without acknowledging God's presence in all aspects of human existence including work, human beings are writing a prescription for anarchy. Unfortunately, some labor leaders, in the midst of a period of culture wars, have taken the side against long-standing religious views despite irrefutable evidence that Americans are a religious people and that Hispanics, including immigrants, are immersed in their faith, albeit all practicing to different degrees. Neither the French Revolution nor communism could stop men and women from practicing their faith or destroy the Catholic Church. The consumerism and materialism that imbues our world today, although more subtle than earlier anti-Christian ideologies, will ultimately have no success either. Each generation ultimately comes to know that by its very nature all humanity comes from the same source, and the lives of human beings are interrelated for good or bad. In the case of Christians, they see the victory as being won and the path clear. All of Catholic social thought teaches Catholics to love God and to love one's neighbor as oneself.

For every argument or theory in the social sciences, one can find refuting cases. Mainline Protestant clergy often support "a women's choice" and same-sex marriages, and the labor movement's social activist arms (e.g., Interfaith Worker Justice) are found to be replete with their numbers.[8] In the Catholic Church, some priests, brothers, and nuns implicitly support or sympathize with these positions through their silence and passivity, but they are not in the Catholic mainstream. Like their liberal Protestant brethren, they do not have the great weight of scripture, Church tradition, or the hierarchical Church leadership to support their role as moral leaders. The recent election of Pope Benedict XVI and the Congregation for Catholic Education's instruction on the Admission of Homosexuals to the Seminary and to Holy Orders have not led to a mass exodus from the Catholic Church. Ethical relativism and subjectivism are not capable of feeding the religious and transcendent longings of people. Catholics, religious and laity, are capable of as much immorality as anyone else, but they also indubitably know right and wrong as others do. While they are susceptible to rationalizing sinful acts, they are also aware that sin exists. When individuals—employers, workers, and religious—recognize their sinfulness, then conversion can happen. This is the starting point. American labor leaders will regain lost ground when the individual and communal conversion occurs. The AFL-CIO's call for a peaceful resolution of the war in Iraq follows this path, but a respect for life and the traditional family as the building block of society are equally important. If such reflection and conversion fail to occur, members and supporters will vote with their feet.

Values Are a Necessary Part of Organizing

Sociologist and labor organizer Paul Johnston contends that all labor scholars attempt to frame their perspective of labor from an "objective outsider" position, which is never an easy feat. Instead, labor scholars should recognize their own philosophical traditions and ideological roots when studying labor and advocating for its role in our society. Labor union research and commentary from a Catholic progressive-conservative position is nearly absent today because too often labor scholars have discounted and stifled Catholic thinking as reactionary. If labor is going to become what theorists label a social movement given present demographics and future trends in the United States, one can argue that Catholic workers, Catholic leaders, and Catholic teaching will have roles to play in the drama. When Johnston speaks of labor unions attempting to provide a broadly-defined "citizenship" to workers in our society, then the Catholic Church has much to offer and Catholic Latinos have much to gain. Catholic social teaching, Catholic parishes, and Catholic schools promote an understanding of citizenship that recognizes all men and women as sons and daughters of God. The efforts of many faithful Catholic Latinos in SEIU, UNITE HERE, the construction trades, on college campuses, and in community organizations have created a smidgen of worker mobilization around living wages, immigration reform, and collective representation. This has occurred because the service economy is expanding and hotels, restaurants, office buildings, and hospitals cannot feasibly move south of the border or offshore. So the successes have happened because culture, language, and ethnicity foster collective action and the employers in the above sectors are vulnerable to organizing. With the support of public sector unions and other viable, progressive unions in the United States as a whole, perhaps the labor movement can engender a new socioeconomic vision that motivates others to organize for the common good. This will not happen, however, if labor concedes to deconstructed and postmodern views that negate God's role in our lives and as a result diminish the importance of respecting all life and the source of new human life, the nuclear family.

Workers engage in concerted activity because of perceived injustices, or they simply leave for other employment.[9] Every working person in a self-reflective moment decides which option is best for him or her. If a person's worklife is stressful and unfulfilling, then change is needed. While most Americans seem to quit such work, others organize to change it.

As far back as the early 1970s, Derek C. Bok and John T. Dunlop in their labor classic, *Labor and the American Community*, saw problems in the house of labor, the historical supporter of worksite organizing:

> Judged by contemporary standards of administration, the typical international union leaves much to be desired. Little effort is devoted to systematic research and long-range planning. Careful procedures for budgeting and resource allocation are virtually unknown. The methods for selecting, training, and motivating officials are often haphazard and not well designed to elevate the ablest, best-trained men to union office. The process of communication up and down the union hierarchy does not produce the information required for formulating and implementing effective policy. And structure of the union is often ill-adapted to the programs of the organization.[10]

In recent years, the AFL-CIO has tried to revitalize its unions, central labor councils, and state federations. This commitment to organizing has resulted in more systematic efforts in the internal reorganizing and external organizing of locals and internationals. System changes, however, do not translate into values that promote wider labor organizing. Labor has yet to connect to the core values of American workers, Latino and non-Latino alike.

Americans are democratic, and they support collective bargaining and employee solidarity in principle. But there is no social movement in labor's house, and some labor intellectuals like Paul Johnston question whether the upsurge of organizing through the late 1930s and into the 1940s was in fact a social movement. It was arguably the conflation of developments in manufacturing, economic volatility, and government support of organizing during that time that led to an approximation of an era of industrial democracy. To this day union leaders and their local memberships guard their autonomy. The AFL-CIO has little influence over the direction of individual unions, and the great majority of members of these unions have seldom had a grand sense of labor solidarity to make them a solidified social and political force within the United States and abroad. No one questions the viability of the unions that recently disaffiliated from the AFL-CIO, which in fact is not one big union. SEIU, UNITE HERE, the Teamsters, the Carpenters Union, and the United Farm Workers (UFW) can all maintain themselves without affiliation and save money for organizing too.[11]

In the United States, context workers in general do not identify with other workers in their job categories nor do they have any evident class consciousness. Furthermore, employers or managers are generally not seen as enemies of the working class because they provide work. Obviously, there is a continuing tension between skilled workers in trades and industrial unions and service workers who work as janitors, hotel staff, and day laborers. These groups don't have much in common in social networks or representational needs.[12] This tension will manifest itself when hotel developers use union labor to build new facilities while committing themselves to maintaining nonunion hotel staffs. The labor movement can assist low-income Latinos and other ethnic groups in gaining representation with recalcitrant low-wage employers, but the labor movement's only real success in the last fifty years at organizing high wage workers came with the advent of public sector collective bargaining. High wage private employers will fight off organizing by providing more of what workers want and passing the cost on to consumers.

In the details of work life, U.S. workers might see individual managers and employers as unjust but they do not see them as an oppressive class. The professional associations that unite intellectual and technical skills are also divided by specialties and interests. In the postmodern world, individuals are failing to work together communally for *the* human good; instead, they pursue their own private goods. Law and moral life were unified in ancient and medieval worlds and provided the framework for cultural and economic development although undeniably injustices and discrimination also occurred in those times. Nevertheless, workers at some primordial level are searching for a unifying effort to do the good.

The practice of virtuous living does not flourish when a society fails to teach and encourage the practice of virtue. And practice, that is, being a good citizen, a good employer, a good worker, requires some respect for authority, a respect for standards, and an acknowledgment of achievement, truthfulness, and fairness. Economic cooperation cannot be achieved unless one practices the moral life mainly for the value of internal goods—doing the right thing because it is right—rather than simply achieving external goods, primarily wealth or material possessions.[13] Virtues, practices, and institutions go together. Institutions contribute to providing the external goods necessary for virtuous practices to flourish. Virtuous living contributes to the establishment of institutions that are necessarily built on trust.

In the United States, collective bargaining is decentralized; consequently, much more bargaining occurs here than in European countries where bargaining is centralized and industry-wide. But the U.S. public tends to reject labor strife and unrest unless it is clearly justifiable. Stopping work is labor's greatest power, but without the sympathy of the public it creates angry consumers, voters, employers, and coworkers. The public responds to those who have a just cause, and maintaining virtuous communal and individual lives are key to effective organizing. Values that promote moral integrity will lead to successful economic organizing.

The Power of Unions in Politics

In both private and public sectors, the interests of unions can cancel out the interests of fellow consumers or taxpayers. But how appropriate are the powers wielded by public sector unions over a few jobs within a much larger economy? Public unions have risen to the top of the labor union heap because of their power in political coalitions and their ability to frame their interests as interests of the public.[14] Does the power of the government itself inordinately strengthen the power of these unions vis-à-vis the taxpayers? Public commentators argue that at times professional bodies like the American Bar Association (ABA) can alter public policy to the detriment of working people, perhaps through unintended consequences. For example, some have reasonably argued that the ABA encourages no-fault divorce laws to the detriment of the family.[15] The mass media which is a part of corporate America has at times parodied and denigrated for profit family and human relationships beyond recognition. Corporate executives have lobbied for a business friendly environment with the goal of maximizing profits and not necessarily social well-being. Yet, public sector unions find themselves in a unique position because their members work for an employer that is highly susceptible to political pressure, the state. In California's November 2005 elections, Governor Arnold Schwarzenegger endorsed Proposition 75 that would have required public sector unions to receive annual written consent from their members to use dues and fees for political work. With an all out labor blitz that included $45 million from unions, the initiative was defeated. In the areas of education, health, and public safety, these unions and their leaders will continue to have a significant influence on the cultural norms ultimately endorsed and promoted across California and the nation.

Do public and private sector unions hold too much influence in elections and therefore public policy? Unions remain the most powerful special interest group within the Democratic Party in a two-party system. In the early years of the AFL, the unions did not have such a fixed alliance with the Democratic Party. In recent years, union leaders, most notably Doug McCarron of the Carpenters Union and James Hoffa of the Teamsters, have sometimes thrown their support behind Republican proposals like Arctic drilling and the construction of nuclear power plants. Although some unions have increased campaign funding to "can't lose" Republican candidates, labor still overwhelmingly supports Democrats. Eighteen of the top twenty Political Action Committee (PAC) contributors to Democratic federal candidates in 2005–2006 were labor unions and seventeen of the top twenty PAC contributors to Republicans were businesses or business associations.[16] On the one hand, Republican union leaders are few and far between; on the other hand, union members will still vote Republican to the chagrin of union officials. In the last two presidential elections, union households made up a quarter of the voters, but a full third of those labor households voted for George W. Bush.[17] Labor's leadership has become a partisan player in its support of the Democratic Party candidates while business PACs seemingly hedge their bets by funding candidates from both parties. If there are no businesses, there are no jobs, which Republican and Democratic politicians alike understand. Moreover in the past, labor's goals were limited in the legislative realm, and they did not stray into nonwork related issues to any great degree. Labor did not venture into culture war minefields like abortion, gun control, or homosexual marriage. With time unions established permanent lobbying offices in state capitols and Washington, D.C., and special interest groups quickly recognized labor's ability to influence politics. Special interest groups have unquestionably influenced the agenda of America's labor leadership.

Unions that promote progressive legislation normally have high numbers of members who will benefit from such efforts. This accounts for many labor leaders supporting social welfare programs during the 1930s when their unskilled members would have benefited from government services. Today, some unions are supporting immigration reform that would assist the large numbers of Hispanics that make up their ranks. Unions, however, are diverse across their own membership and across labor. American workers and unions experience different benefits and costs due to immigration. Quite naturally, the primary supporters of immigration reform are SEIU, UNITE HERE, and building trades unions that have large Latino memberships. The Internet, however, is full of debates among union members about the loss of jobs to immigrants.

In the public sector, one finds local, county, and state public sector unions in relationship with elected officials to further political agendas that are mutually supportive. Government leaders are not hard bargainers especially when their election to office depends on the support of public sector employees and their unions. But it is important to note that wages and benefits, particularly pensions, make up a significant percentage of state and local government expenditures. Politicians come and go but public sector workers remain, and the leaders of public unions are influential in shaping the culture and politics in all fifty states. If civil servants have the commonly accepted academic credentials and the government through its bureaucratic machinery directs a community's resources, the average citizen's role in politics becomes less of a concern. Alasdair McIntyre contends that the same "competence" and "resource-control" argument is made by private industry. Bureaucracies emerge and their managers make decisions based on their purported expertise in the social/managerial sciences. Yet they rely on ostensible value neutrality and claims to manipulative power, which others can rightfully call into question.[18] The generalizations developed from the social sciences normally have refuting counter examples and are more often than not only probabilistic in their validity. Public school teachers may know how to teach but when it comes to values, they might not teach what parents want their children to learn. This becomes problematic when unions and their academic advisors become proponents of anti-Catholic and/or anti-Latino positions and values.

Lobbying, referenda, and direct public appeals are the tools of public unions. The state's employee relations issues are open for everyone to see and when the state accepts collective bargaining, the people's sovereignty is necessarily hamstrung by the bargaining rights of employees. If an administrator cannot negotiate an equitable agreement with the public sector union, the union can then go directly to the administration or legislature. Proposition 75 in California recently attempted to tighten the control over the use of public sector union members' political contributions to unions that at times may not authentically represent many members' beliefs. Perhaps using a neutral panel to make a contract recommendation to a government executive and/or legislature is one means of reaching a collective bargaining agreement. The politics of the situation will never end, however, because panel members are political appointees. State and local governments could also prevent unequal salaries and benefits by negotiating across job categories rather than bargaining for firefighters, clerical workers, police officers, prison guards, and others as individual bargaining units.

Most public jobs concern safety and health, and citizens do not want prolonged strikes that jeopardize these public goods. But public sector unions can expect a public backlash if voters perceive them as too much of a self-interested, special interest group. While Proposition 75 was defeated, the recall of California Governor Gray Davis was in part due to the perceived negative influence of public unions in his administration. Teachers, firefighters, and police officers, although they have important jobs in our society, are not underpaid farmworkers. The justice issue rings hollow if they have more time off, better wages, and superior health benefits than the average private sector worker. In the end, public sector unions, or at least their leaders, will maintain broad-based goodwill by remaining neutral on controversial non-job related political issues.

Immigration Reform

On January 7, 2004, President Bush proposed a new temporary worker program. His intent was to create a more humane immigration system that would replace the underground labor market, which placed undocumented workers in a precarious state. Many immigrant workers have been working without health, safety, and income protections. He also acknowledged the contributions that earlier immigrants had made to the success of American society as workers, military personnel, and entrepreneurs, and he underscored the moral force that immigrants provide to our society. "They bring to America the values of faith in God, love of family, hard work and self-reliance—the values that made us a great nation to begin with." He admitted that American workers often do not take many jobs in the U.S. economy and that documented and undocumented immigrants have filled this need. "Out of common sense and fairness, our laws should allow willing workers to enter our country and fill jobs that Americans are not filling. We must make our immigration laws more rational, and more humane. And I believe we can do so without jeopardizing the livelihoods of American citizens." Furthermore, in a time of terrorist threats, the borders into the United States have to stop both terrorists and criminals from entering the United States.

President Bush's answer is to strengthen the U.S. borders by creating a strong system for tracking the whereabouts of legal visitors and offering temporary (only three years) but renewable legal status to foreign workers who staff positions that Americans are not filling. Host employers will have the responsibility of providing work data on these temporary employees, and the employees will receive temporary worker cards that give them the freedom to travel back and forth to their homelands. As an incentive for them to return to their own countries, the Bush administration has suggested that they contribute, with the assistance of the United States, to their nation's pension program as well as tax-preferred savings accounts.

This is not an amnesty program. Temporary workers who wish to become U.S. citizens have to complete and pass the normal naturalization process. While criticized by a few Republicans, the proposal is one of fairness and decency. It is not a draconian response to immigration that is based on economics or a proposal that denies national sovereignty.[19]

In November 2005, President Bush repeated this message of immigration reform at Tucson, Arizona, and underscored the importance of securing the U.S. border. While the border must encourage trade and foreign visitors, the U.S. government should have the capacity to weed out terrorists and criminals. He called for Congress to work with him to sign a comprehensive immigration reform bill by 2006. The latest version of his reform initiative includes the repatriation of illegal entrants deeper into Mexico which in recent trial cases has discouraged 92 percent of these non-documented Mexicans from making further attempts at illegal entry. In addition, the federal government plans to increase the number of beds at detention centers by 10 percent and expedite the return of undocumented foreigners. Federal officials will work to decrease the number of illegal entrants who are released for future court appearances because too many undocumented foreigners fail to make their court appearances. The federal government has increased the number of border agents from 9,500 to 12,500 since 2001, purchased $139 million in unmanned aerial vehicles for surveillance, infrared cameras and other border enforcement tools, and made $70 million worth of border barriers and infrastructure changes to prevent illegal crossings. On the American citizen side of the illegal immigration issue, President Bush is increasing work site enforcement of employment laws, improving detection of document fraud, and beefing up the number of immigration investigators by four hundred in 2006. In Tucson the President reiterated his plan for a temporary worker program that would allow foreign nationals to work temporarily in the United States. With temporary I.D. cards, men and women who are working to serve their families can contribute to the economic growth of the country, and prospective permanent citizens will have to start at the beginning in the application process.

Immigrants play a vital role in strengthening American democracy. This is a land in which foreigners who respect the laws are welcomed as contributors to American culture and not feared as threats. The United States has been strengthened by generations of immigrants who became Americans through patience, hard work, and assimilation. Like previous generations of immigrants, every new citizen has an obligation to learn this nation's customs and values. At the same time, America will fulfill its obligation to give each citizen a chance to realize the American dream. By enforcing immigration laws, the federal government is protecting the promise of a tolerant, welcoming America and preserving opportunity for all.[20]

The U.S. Conference of Catholic Bishops has endorsed the Secure America and Orderly Immigration Act (S. 1033, HR 2330). Senators John McCain and Edward Kennedy introduced it in the Senate, and Representatives Jim Kolbe, Jeff Flake, and Luis Gutierrez introduced it in the House of Representatives. This plan is clearly more liberal than the president's proposal because it would provide an expedited process for giving permanent status to illegal immigrants in the United States and simplify family reunification. These undocumented workers would have to pay a fine for coming to the United States illegally, but the government would help them legalize their status. In other words, punishing those who are here illegally but at the same time caring for these workers and their families in a humane manner. Some argue that any guest worker plan leaves all the power in the hands of employers who can manipulate immigration status to their benefit. They could threaten guest workers with discharge or play nonimmigrants against immigrants. The Association of Community Organizations for Reform Now (ACORN) supports the Secure America and Orderly Immigration Act and has already held meetings and rallies to promote its passage.[21] Other supporters include: The Farm Labor Organizing Committee (FLOC), the Jesuit Conference and Jesuit Refugee Service, the Laborers International Union of North America (LIUNA), the Mexican-American Legal Defense and Educational Fund (MALDEF), SEIU, UFW, and the U.S. Chamber of Commerce. Nevertheless, union members like the rest of American society are divided on the issue of illegal immigration.

At a January 2006 Immigration Alert Forum hosted by Teamsters Local 952 in Orange County, California, many union representatives and immigrant activists expressed concern with each immigration reform proposal then in Congress. The Teamsters Union had not endorsed the Kennedy-McCain legislation because the guest worker provision "undermines unionization and the ability to improve good wages and working conditions." David Bacon, a noted labor activist and journalist, called for a rejection of both proposals before Congress because of the harm that each would cause. He advocated a common ground proposal created by labor, Latinos, and African-Americans. Such a proposal would promote immigration reform, civil rights, and jobs. Unfortunately, given the importance of religious groups in the immigration debate, no recognized officials of religious groups nor their representatives participated in the forum.[22]

Mondragón

The ardent Catholic Philip Murray, the United Steelworkers of America (USWA) president in the 1940s and the early 1950s, was a great fan of "industry councils." He envisioned councils where workers and managers would codetermine the production procedures and administration in the shop, at the factory, and across an industry. The idea was a natural development from the corporatism espoused in the Catholic social encyclical *Quadragismo Anno* and centuries old Catholic proclivities for the organic solidarity of the medieval guild system. Workers and managers support each other in wages, benefits, and working conditions while providing products and services to others. During World War II, labor-management committees were formed in industrial settings, often with the encouragement of Catholic labor priests and Catholic labor leaders, but they failed. Apparently management and labor could never move beyond their misgivings about each other's goals. Unions have contributed to employee-management relationships in the United States because many of them have promoted employee-participation efforts, a form of internal corporate jurisprudence through the development of grievance procedures, wage policies, and benefits that have become the standard for nonunion workplaces. But as far as changing the nature of worklife they have had much less influence because they are not oriented toward the meaning and quality of work nor are they the ultimate employers. The one who has the power to hire and fire has the ultimate authority over the quality of worklife, but this authority also faces the exigencies of the market system. In an employment-at-will economy, labor unions are unquestionably the best job protection available to a worker. Nonetheless, Catholics have perennially struggled with the confrontational nature of collective bargaining because it assumes a position of division rather than solidarity. In other words, the division between capital and labor is a false dichotomy; fundamentally, God did not create divisions between people. For example, Catholic Worker leaders Peter Maurin and Dorothy Day believed that all human beings were meant to find fulfillment and dignity in their work. They felt that industrial relations based on confrontational collective bargaining failed to achieve this ideal and therefore promoted agricultural cooperatives and communal living in their own Catholic Worker movement.

Labor theorists have long imagined industrial and service organizations that are built as cooperatives where the workers are owners/employers. In the last fifty years, the Mondragón Cooperative Corporation in the Basque region of Spain has provided the world with the best example of a sophisticated, viable worker-owned enterprise. The 1986 Catholic bishop's pastoral letter *Economic Justice for All* contains a chapter entitled "A New American Experiment: Partnership for the Public Good." This section includes a footnote to the Harvard Business School Case Study, "The Mondragón Cooperative Movement," written by David Ellerman. Many Catholics interested in economic issues look to Mondragón as a viable model for economic development. Officials in the Catholic bishops' Campaign for Human Development have visited Mondragón and in 1992, the year before he died, César Chávez visited Mondragón as well.[23]

Don Jose María Arizmendirrieta, a Catholic diocesan priest, with the help of area residents, founded the cooperative which currently employs over 70,000 people worldwide, half of whom are worker-owners.[24] Although early in his religious life Don José María wanted to study sociology at the Louvain in Belgium, his bishop assigned him in 1941 to Mondragón to work as a parish priest. The people were desperately poor during the post–Spanish Civil War years. Like a good community organizer, he circulated among the people of the town to learn from them the nature of their needs. In effect, he engaged in community organizing through one-on-one interviews. Community members first proposed building a playing field, a rather innocuous request. Don José María then went about gathering the resources and labor to build the field and later a medical clinic. He organized a youth group and the parish families through these efforts.

After their initial successes, Don José María found that his working class community wanted better education for its sons and daughters (primarily sons at that time) so that they could find employment in the future. He organized a parents' association which began to petition employers for funds to start a technical school and also solicited funds from other community members. At one point, street corners in Mondragón held large boxes where people could drop cards with their names, addresses, and pledge amounts, or offers of other forms of support. Those who contributed to the "dream school" received the right to vote on policy decisions for what then become the Escuela Politénica Profesional. At one point Don José María's superiors had to ask him to soften his democratic initiatives for fear of reprisals from the Franco government, but Mondragón's history shows that the people built their community association and industrial cooperative all within the bounds of Spanish law and government.[25]

As the first children progressed in the Escuela Politénica Profesional, the school expanded to higher grades until it reached the point of granting undergraduate degrees in cooperation with a university in a neighboring province.[26] As the students learned their technical skills, Don José was inculcating them with his social vision that he learned from the writings of

Robert Owen, who had promoted cooperatives in Britain and the United States in the nineteenth century, and Catholic social doctrine. Some of the first students recall that the better part of his religion classes were discussions in sociology.[27] In many ways Don José María was a priest who had an avocation as an applied sociologist. One can assume that his religion classes were really about religion but with an emphasis on how men and women in a Christian community might live in an industrial world. Would they live by self-centered individualism or would they cooperate with each other to deal with the vagaries of a world that necessarily responds to market demands? The parish priest never hesitated in criticizing both capitalism and socialism:

> The third way of development equidistant from individualist capitalism and soulless collectivism [is cooperativism]. Its center and axis is the human person in his social context.
>
> It is the third way distinct from egoist capitalism and from the mastodon of depersonalizing socialism. We want cooperatives which constitute a new social potential and, thus, are built by those who are not impelled by a myopic and limited egotism or by a simple gregarious instinct.
>
> The cooperativist distinguishes himself from the capitalist, simply in that the latter utilizes capital in order to make people serve him, while the former uses it to make more gratifying and uplifting the working life of the people.[28]

Five of the Escuela Politénica Profesional's first graduates with Don José María's encouragement proposed a plan for the worker-ownership of area companies. After being rejected by employers and the Spanish government, the teacher and his disciples went to their supporters in the community and raised about $365,000 in 1955 dollars. The group bought a bankrupt company that had a valuable state license to produce electrical appliances for homes. The students and the visionary priest called the cooperative Ulgor, a combination of the initials of the students' names.[29]

The founders drew up a constitution which created a governing council whose members would be elected by all the workers. Each worker continues to have one vote. The manager of Ulgor and of the subsequent cooperatives is the equivalent of a CEO, and he or she is under the control of a general council and only has a voice in council proceedings. The governing council fulfills the function of management while a social council is in a sense the advocate of the members as workers. Clearly, all participants are managers and workers. The social council is used as an advocate, although not a union, for better safety, fair compensation, improved benefits, and so on. When serious work-related problems arise, the social council can call a general assembly of the members to discuss and vote on the manner of proceeding. A general assembly is held annually.[30]

Members are not stockholders because the cooperative does not trade in its ownership. Members join the cooperative by paying a membership fee of a few thousand dollars when new workers are needed. The cooperative compensates its members at a rate that is slightly better than the Spanish average for all job categories. The profit (which is sales minus costs of labor, materials, and other normal expenses) is divided among members according to the hours they have worked and their compensation level (basically, their job category). The profit is placed into an account established for each member. The member may only withdraw the interest earned on the account until he or she leaves the cooperative at which time the principal is paid to the former member. Most importantly, one's account cannot be transferred to others.[31]

To say the least, Mondragón has been quite a success. The cooperative now operates the sixteenth largest bank in Spain (Caja Laboral Popular) and it, too, is run as a cooperative. The cooperative complex had assets of $14 billion and sales of $8 billion in 2004.[32] Many new cooperatives have spun off from the original Ulgor, so that today Mondragón has cooperatives that range from agriculture production to semiconductor fabrication. From the agriculture production, a chain of supermarkets developed. It also has a research and development organization that is run as a cooperative while being financed by the other cooperatives. And, of course, many of Mondragón's members live in cooperative housing and send their children to cooperative day care centers. One finds that cooperatives developed because they were a means of import substitution. Each new cooperative provided a natural service to pre-existing cooperatives. To go full circle, schools are financed by the cooperatives, and Alecop, its showcase school, provides a half a day of schooling and a half a day of work for its students. Alecop is run as a cooperative and, therefore, prepares its students for futures as full-fledged Mondragón members.[33]

Over time Mondragón has been restructured to make accommodations for its size, but the basic roles of the social council and governing council remain the same. In 1974, a strike occurred among some members over production rules but it was soon settled. As a result of the strike, the constitution was amended to give members the right to form unions, but up to this date unions have not generated much interest. Similarly, members can bring their political views to any situation or discussion, but the cooperatives do not endorse any party or candidate. The cooperative has been successful because as changes become necessary, the social council acts as an influential force in decision making. Surely no association of human beings is perfect. North American social scientists have criticized the cooperative for being weighted too heavily on technical matters rather than social ones,[34] and some visitors have complained of hazardous working conditions. In addition, as the cooperative has grown, the members have had to process greater amounts of information. Don José María felt that it would always be necessary to socialize knowledge to democratize power. This becomes difficult with increases in the complexity of the organization. Yet the founder always insisted on constant reevaluation of the cooperative's efforts, so Mondragón may very well overcome this problem as well.

Don José María's goal was nothing less than a transformation of society, which at its roots is a religious endeavor. His religion, however, was not one of Spanish mysticism but Basque pragmatism, and he traveled on a different thoroughfare in the city of religion than many of his contemporaries. Alfonso Gorroñogoitia, one of the cooperative's founding members, explains how the master taught them:

> We were disciples who year after year educated ourselves, thanks to the teachings of Don José María, along lines of social concerns and toward a translation of religious ideas into something that would link up with our real world. Don José María imbued us with the idea that being a man meant to occupy one's self and do something. That is taken for granted now, but in those days there was a spiritual, scholastic, and puristic atmosphere in the Church. In other places, Acción Católica taught different ideas, people dedicated themselves to Castilian mysticism. Don José María was different in that he was telling us that men have problems and must work in the building of their world. From Don José María I learned that work was not a punishment—which I had been taught earlier—but rather the realization of the Creation and collaboration with the plan of God. . . .
>
> Thanks to the establishment of the Escuela Profesional, we developed the idea that in order to do things we needed technical competence as well as *spiritual witness and personal effort* [emphasis added].[35]

Gorroñogoitia explains that other business people see the difference that religious values have played in Mondragón's success:

> What surprises other entrepreneurs is the poetic-philosophic vein that we have as entrepreneurs. This humanistic inclination that surprises them we owe to Don José María, because we could never dissociate our entrepreneurial attitudes from a philosophy, a concept, an ideology, after the contact we had with him. We could not be pure technocrats, who know perfectly the

processes of chemistry or physics or semi-conductors but nothing more. We have never been pure technocrats. We see the development of these firms as a social struggle, a duty.[36]

Don José María studied the Catholic social encyclicals, and their ideas resonated with him. He and his students put them into action. He also read widely, e.g., the works of French-Catholic philosophers Jacques Maritain and Emmanuel Mounier who influenced the Catholic Worker movement, and he often used Marxian criticisms of capitalism in his teaching. However, he never supported armed insurrections as did radical Basque groups.[37] He also criticized the Catholic Church for alienating working people although he always remained a faithful Catholic priest.

Don José María often said, "We have recognized that theory is necessary, yes, but it is not sufficient: we build the road as we travel."[38] He believed that as problems arose the cooperative members as an industrial community would evaluate solutions and come to some consensus as to the best route to take. When mistakes are made, new solutions will be sought. The Mondragón member is not born as a cooperator but the fellow members teach each the values of the cooperative. The Basque priest remarked:

> One is not born a cooperator, because to be a cooperator requires a social maturity, a training in social living. For one to be an authentic cooperator, capable of cooperating, it is necessary to have learned to tame one's individualistic or egoistic instincts and to adapt to the laws of cooperation. . . .
> One becomes a cooperator through education and the practice of virtue.[39]

> To teach only how men should behave with each other, without attacking their egotism, is like plowing in the sea. . . . Before teaching them public relations and courtesy, we have to get them accustomed to forgetting about themselves.[40]

Mondragón offers a model for economic development through job creation. Given the network of Catholic colleges and universities in the United States and the guidance of U.S. Catholic bishops, local organizers, labor unions, academics, immigrants, and students should be incubating worker-owned enterprises. In fact, the Catholic Bishops' Campaign for Human Development has supported U.S. cooperative ventures for decades. The Campaign for Human Development has provided, however, too little financial capital and no managerial support. The bishops could create an economic development corporation that is specifically designed to focus on cooperatives. The corporation would be nonprofit and have the financial resources to attract the money, talent, and skills to act as a business incubator. The cooperative ventures would then have a pool of resources, e.g., both accounting and legal skills, which would be purchased at a reasonable rate. Catholic universities and colleges are full of young, idealistic, and talented students who are open to a different way of living and working. Faith and religion were significant variables in the success of Mondragón because people of humility and goodwill, recognizing their talents and deficiencies, put aside self-centeredness to serve one another. They created work out of the social, intellectual, political, and most importantly spiritual capital that they had at hand, and this is the key to Mondragón's success. The schools that Don José María helped found taught technical expertise and Christian values. Through the education of the youth, Don José María laid the groundwork for a cooperative culture that has had some notable success. The Mondragón Cooperative Corporation currently has over one hundred cooperatives and is Spain's third largest exporter. All of this was done in just over fifty years.

Mondragón workers do not obstruct the introduction of technology into the workplace, and they have no reason to featherbed because they are seeking returns on their investment in the company. Communal indifference is not going to happen because of the missionary ethos that the cooperative generates and the loyalty of the members. The members accept wage differentials based on expertise, contributions, difficulty of a task, and merit. The cooperative provides its own training and education, now including one of the best engineering schools in Spain. While U.S. employers seek motivation and loyalty through stock ownership plans, profit sharing initiatives, and quality circles (i.e., participative management), Mondragón members are tied to their company by ownership and this capitalizes on self-interest.

Mondragón is about human dignity, human solidarity, and subsidiarity at the work site and in the community. Mondragón's administration does not constantly shop in the external labor market for employees and managers in a world that some say calls for flexibility in the employee pool; rather, it offers a counter example to the disposable worker phenomenon. Education and training happens within the cooperative. While some might fear an insular community with a paternalistic flavor, others might value the stability and security that the cooperative community provides while recognizing the challenges of industrial democracy.

Finding capital has always been a concern for fledgling worker-owned enterprises. Labor in the past has tried to create an ongoing source of financial capital and to serve union depositors at labor banks. Yet, labor banks in the United States have failed because of nepotism, a lack of managerial skills, insufficient knowledge of the finance industry, and a fear on the part of members in supporting these institutions. While recognizing the admirable goal of establishing labor banks in the 1920s, Dunlop and Bok report that most of them failed by the 1930s. "It reveals the danger of falling prey too quickly to the romantic visions put forward by those who so often urge unions to experiment along radically different lines. Labor banks also point up the problems that can arise when unions engage in complex ventures beyond their natural function of representing employees."[41] Yet, the possibility and opportunity still exists. Labor could work with local schools of higher education to create jobs by nurturing new businesses. Some unions like the Sheet Metal Workers International Association (SMWIA) already support member-owner businesses. Union pension plans have money for investment, another source of financial capital to support economic development if a community has set goals for education, industry development, and job creation. Clearly, a venture into worker-ownership supported by labor unions, Catholics, immigrants, and others of goodwill would require energy, talent, and spiritual capital to achieve success.

Latinos, the Catholic Church, and Labor

While the government has taken on some of the functions of unions and employers by setting wages and conditions for the workplace, government standards normally set out minimum requirements, and workers and their supporters will necessarily debate the adequacy and justice of minimum levels. George P. Shultz, former U.S. Secretary of State, Labor, and Treasury, has commented that a nation is never truly free without viable labor unions to represent the concerns of workers. The labor organizing of Catholic Latinos offers another opportunity to keep the United States economically strong and politically free. Recent immigrants, whether documented or undocumented, are fresh blood for the United States. They are arguably contributing more benefits than costs to the U.S. economy, but more importantly are worthy of dignified lives as sons and daughters of God, no matter their ethnicity, race, national origin, or creed.

Labor unions must, however, organize where the people are at and not where a cadre of liberal activists wants them to be. If labor is to strengthen its role in American society, then citizens and noncitizens alike must identify with unions for organizing, effective union governance, collective bargaining, and planning. Labor groups need an ethos that promotes employers, customers, and workers, which is a path that is not solely focused on gains for the membership. Self-interest is appropriate, but self-centeredness does not lead to new growth. The efforts of the workers are seen as a bigger whole—greater than any one union—that is related to the entire society. Membership brings meaning and pride to participants. Great construction projects of past civilizations, the study of science, the development of the arts, and the appreciation of sports (e.g., the Olympic Games) grew out of "cult" thereby creating culture.

Human work and achievement have meaning when they are directed to God and for Catholic workers, the liturgy and work life go together. The word "liturgy" means public service, that is, "work of the people." The ritual celebration of the sacraments presents the evangelical tension between cult and ethics. French theologian Louis-Marie Chauvet writes:

> The element "Sacrament" is thus the symbolic place of the ongoing transition between Scripture and Ethics, from the letter to the body. The liturgy is the powerful pedagogy where we learn to consent to the presence of the absence of God who obliges us to give him a body in the world, thereby giving the sacraments their plenitude in the "liturgy of the neighbor" and giving the ritual memory of Jesus Christ its plenitude in our existential memory.[42]

Faithful Catholics recognize this dynamic and have participated in it for centuries. Hospitals and schools are two community institutions that were born of the work of the word of God made present in the world by the faithful. In fact, health care labor unions and teachers unions should consider greater collaboration with Catholic Church officials to promote accessible health care and better education in the United States. One would expect health care workers to stand for a respect for life; it is their vocation. The voucher dilemma would be less of an issue if Church officials were neutral with regard to the organizing of their schools and if the unions supported vouchers to pay for at least some of the costs of Catholic parochial education. In a pluralistic society, the state should not penalize parents who wish to send their children to accredited religious-affiliated schools. The day-to-day organizing efforts of Catholic Latinos and Catholic Latino immigrants are woven throughout the fabric of U.S. labor history. Catholic religious and laymen and women have contributed to the rise of labor unions, fought against their fall, and continue to promote their success. The Catholic Church is an institutional ally in the organizing of Latinos and all other peoples who are in need. Labor unions and their allies will find greater success in their efforts if they recognize the legitimacy of Catholic concerns for the family and life when they reach out to this invaluable supporter.

Notes

1. *What's At Stake? Help 57 million workers gain a union*, http://www.unionvoice.org/campaign/Support_EFCA/explanation (visited Oct. 5, 2005).

2. Derek C. Bok and John T. Dunlop, *Labor and the American Community* (New York: Simon and Schuster, 1970), 213.

3. Joann Wypijewski, "The New Unity Partnership: A Manifest Destiny for Labor," *Counterpunch*, http://www.counterpunch.org/jw10062003.html, Oct. 6, 2003 (visited Jan. 26, 2006).

4. SEIU has already faced a backlash by its membership in its own streamlining efforts. Immigrant janitors in SEIU Local 87 (San Francisco, Calif.) fought SEIU's move to consolidate the union with Local 1877. Some of the San Francisco janitors decertified the union but have now reaffiliated after receiving major concessions for local autonomy by the international. Some Bay area paramedics and emergency medical technicians attempted to decertify SEIU Local 250 at American Medical Response Co., but Local 250 averted decertification when the vote ended in a draw. Local union members will fight for democracy in their unions when national unions officials attempt to consolidate power without their consent.

5. Joann Wypijewski, "The New Unity Partnership: A Manifest Destiny for Labor."

6. Ibid.

7. See *Deus est Caritas*, Pope Benedict XVI, Jan. 2006.

8. Don Lattin, "Pushing poverty into 'moral-values' debate, Some religious leaders trying to broaden discussion beyond abortion and marriage," *San Francisco Chronicle*, A-1, Dec. 12, 2004.

9. Ibid., 76.

10. Bok and Dunlop, 186.

11. See Miriam Pawel, "UFW: A Broken Contract (1 of 4), Farmworkers Reap Little as Union Strays From Its Root," *Los Angeles Times*, http://www.latimes.com/news/local/la-me-ufw8jan08,1,7202033.story?coll=la-headlines-california (visited Jan. 12, 2006).
The UFW has had little success at organizing farmworkers and has refocused the capital accumulated under César Chávez' name to serving the U.S. Latino population in housing developments, political lobbying, and radio broadcasting. The union is a political organization with a social calling.

12. Henry Katz, "Whither the America Labor Movement," in Lowell Turner, Harry C. Katz, and Richard W. Hurd, eds., *Rekindling the Movement: Labor's Quest for Relevance in the 21st Century* (Ithaca, N.Y.: ILR Press, 2001), 344.

13. Alasdair MacIntyre, *After Virtue* (Notre Dame, Ind.: University of Notre Dame Press, 1984).

14. Paul Johnston, "Organizing for What: The Resurgence of Labor as a Citizenship Movement," in Lowell Turner, Harry C. Katz, and Richard W. Hurd, eds., *Rekindling the Movement: Labor's Quest for Relevance in the 21st Century* (Ithaca, N.Y.: ILR Press, 2001), 44.

15. David R. Usher, *Divorce and Bankruptcy Reform*, http://www.mensnewsdaily .com/archive/u-v/usher/2005/usher030905.htm (visited Dec. 22, 2005).

16. Center for Responsive Politics, *Top PACs*, http://www.opensecrets.org/pacs/ topacs.asp (visited Dec. 26, 2005).

17. Leigh Strope, "Despite massive effort and spending, unions couldn't deliver votes for Kerry," *San Francisco Chronicle*, http://sfgate.com/cgi-bin/article.cgi?file=/ news/archive/2004/11/04/politics0306EST0431.DTL (visited Nov. 4, 2004).

18. MacIntyre, 86.

19. *President Bush Proposes New Temporary Worker Program*, Presidential Speech, Jan. 7, 2004, http://www.whitehouse.gov/news/releases/2004/01/20040107-3.html (visited Dec. 12, 2005).

20. *Fact Sheet: Securing America Through Immigration Reform*, Press Release, The White House, President George W. Bush, http://www.whitehouse.gov/news/releases/ 2005/11/20051128-3.html (visited Dec. 14, 2005).

21. *Secure America and Orderly Immigration Act*, ACORN.org, http://acorn.org/ index.php?id=9317 (visited Dec. 14, 2005).

22. *Immigration Alert Forum Teamsters Local 952*, Orange, Calif., Jan. 21, 2006, e-mail correspondence in author's position, dbacon@igc.org.

23. Christopher Zehnder, "We're More Than Just Farm Workers: The UFW and Catholicism," *Los Angeles Lay Catholic Mission* (April 1997), 4.

24. Not all are worker-owners due to restrictive legislation in some foreign countries, others are part-timers before becoming worker-owners, and still other non-member employees work at distant distribution sites.

25. William Whyte and Kathleen Whyte, *Making Mondragón: The Growth and Dynamics of the Worker Cooperative Complex* (Ithaca, N.Y.: ILR Press, 1991), 30.

26. Ibid., 32.

27. Jesus Larrañaga *Buscando un camino: Don Jose Maria Arizmendi-Arrieta y la Experiencia Cooperativa de Mondragón* (Bilbao, Spain: R&F, 1981), 777. Quoted in William Whyte and Kathleen Whyte, *Making Mondragón*, 253.

28. Larrañaga 1981, 757.

29. William Whyte and Kathleen Whyte, *Making Mondragón*, 34.

30. Ibid., 37.

31. Ibid., 43.

32. Mondragón Corporación Cooperativa, http://www.mondragon.mcc.es/ing/ magnitudes/cifras.html (visited Jan. 23, 2006).

33. William Whyte and Kathleen Whyte, *Making Mondragón*, 54.

34. Ibid., 220.

35. Ibid., 245.

36. Ibid., 245.

37. Ibid., 247.

38. Larrañaga, *Buscando un Camnio*, 481. Quoted Whyte and Whyte, *Making Mondragón*, 257.

39. Ibid., 231. Quoted in Whyte and Whyte, *Making Mondragón*, 256.

40. Ibid., 245. Quoted in Whyte and Whyte, *Making Mondragón*, 259.

41. Bok and Dunlop, 368.

42. Louis-Marie Chauvet, *Symbol and Sacrament: A Sacramental Reinterpretation of Christian Experience*, translated by Patrick Madigan, SJ, and Madeleine Beaumont (Collegeville, Minn.: The Liturgical Press, 1995), 265.

Index

~

About the Author

George E. Schultze, SJ, studied Industrial and Labor Relations at Cornell University, completed an MBA at the University of California, Berkeley, and received his doctorate in Social Ethics at the University of Southern California. Prior to entering the Society of Jesus, he worked for the National Labor Relations Board. He has published articles about work life and Catholic social thought and is presently Professor and Spiritual Director at St. Patrick's Seminary and University in Menlo Park, California.